RESTORED IN THE RUINS

Darlene Mullins
6414 Ashmore Lane
Tyler, Texas 75703

Restored in the Ruins

VICKI LAKE

VICTOR BOOKS®
A DIVISION OF SCRIPTURE PRESS PUBLICATIONS INC.
USA CANADA ENGLAND

Copyediting: LaMoyne Schneider
Cover Design: Mardelle Ayres
Cover (Fabric) Design © 1990 Courtesy of and supplied by John Kaldor Fabricmaker USA, Ltd.
Cover Photo: William Koechling

Recommended Dewey Decimal Classification: 222.8
Suggested Subject Heading: BIBLE, O.T., NEHEMIAH

Library of Congress Catalog Card Number: 91-68131
ISBN: 0-89693-877-8

1 2 3 4 5 6 7 8 9 10 Printing/Year 96 95 94 93 92

VICTOR BOOKS
A division of SP Publications, Inc.
Wheaton, Illinois 60187

CONTENTS

INTRODUCTION

Do you sometimes panic and feel powerless when confronted with seemingly insurmountable problems? Is your life so disorganized that even an efficiency expert would run for cover? Have you forgotten how to praise God? If so, this study of the Book of Nehemiah is for *you*.

In today's society, we often look for the quickest and easiest route of escape when facing problems. We expect solutions as instantly as microwave delicacies. Some problems are easy to solve, but then there are the others. . . . Nehemiah faced the difficult kind when he found he himself was the answer to his own prayer of concern over the broken-down walls of Jerusalem and the broken-down wills of the Jews living there.

During this study, we'll observe how Nehemiah confronted problems, organized efficiently, mobilized workers, and praised God. We'll also see God's power at work in spiritually reviving the disobedient Jews. Most of all, we'll see God's power demonstrated as the Jews pulled together to complete the rebuilding of the Jerusalem walls in a miraculous 52 days—and this in the face of opposition. Even the Jews' enemies attested indirectly in Nehemiah 6:15-16 to God's power: "So the wall was completed on the twenty-fifth of Elul, in fifty-two days. When all our enemies heard about this, all the surrounding nations were afraid and lost their self-confidence, because they realized that *this work had been done with the help of our God*" (emphasis added). Realizing the possibility and reality of God's power for our daily lives could be the best principle you gain from this study of the Book of Nehemiah.

Each study of this book is divided into sections. *Gathering the Materials* will enable you to do an inductive study of the Book of

Nehemiah. *Laying the Foundation*, a narrative section, will explain and enlarge some spiritual concepts introduced in the inductive section. *Adding Reinforcement* is a special section which gives practical pointers for prayer. Lastly, *Maintaining Daily Upkeep* is a journaling section intended to help you begin or maintain the daily disciplines of reading, applying, and memorizing God's Word.

If you are studying on your own, make a point of sharing what you are learning with someone else. You will solidify lessons in your mind while blessing your friend.

If you are part of a group, you will find it most helpful to work through the study questions on your own before the group meets. Then you will be ready to share what you learned from the passage and how it applies to your life, plus any questions that arose as you studied. Members will profit from hearing one another's insights and perceptions.

Using the inductive study questions, work through the Scripture passage *before* you read the narrative section; in this way, your initial findings will all be original.

Throughout the study, remember that the Holy Spirit is your teacher. Ask Him to give you eyes to see His truth, and a spirit ready to obey it.

As you come across questions that call for you to connect the truth of the passage to your own life, answer them prayerfully. Let the Spirit guide you in applying God's Word to your life. When you find something in the passage that makes you feel grateful to God, thank Him! When something leads you to praise Him, stop and do so! When the Spirit points to something in your life that doesn't measure up to what you're reading in Scripture, let Him speak to you. Confess any sin and allow God to cleanse you and lead you in the right direction.

To be properly equipped for each study, you will need this study guide, your favorite Bible translation (the study is based on the *New International Version*), plus any other materials named by the leader (if you have one). You might want a notebook in which to record your thoughts, discoveries, or questions from studying. You could also use it to list and date personal or group prayer requests, plus their resolutions.

PRAYING PURPOSEFULLY

❧

GATHERING THE MATERIALS

Read Nehemiah 1.
1. Where is Nehemiah, and what is he doing?

2. What does Nehemiah learn about the remnant of Jews and the city of Jerusalem? How did he react?

How do you react when burdened with a need or a cause?

For whom or what have you been most burdened recently?

3. Read the passages below; then tell how you think the words of leaders and prophets who ministered before Nehemiah affected his prayers.

   ❧ Deuteronomy 30:1-4

   ❧ Jeremiah 29:10-14

   ❧ Jeremiah 33:6-9

   ❧ Zechariah 4:6-10

4. Choose from the following words to describe the various sections of Nehemiah's prayer in 1:5-11: penitence, promises, praise, and petition.

1:5 _____ 1:8-10 _____

1:6-7 _____ 1:11 _____

5. Describe the character of God, according to Nehemiah's prayer.

   How do the following verses describe Him?
   - ❦ Numbers 14:17-19
   - ❦ Deuteronomy 3:24; 7:9
   - ❦ 1 Chronicles 29:11
   - ❦ 1 Corinthians 1:9
   - ❦ 2 Thessalonians 3:3

6. What sins did Nehemiah confess?

   According to the verses below, why was and is confession important?
   - ❦ 2 Chronicles 7:14
   - ❦ Psalm 32:1-6
   - ❦ Proverbs 28:13
   - ❦ Romans 4:4-8
   - ❦ 1 John 1:9

   Are there any sins in your life which you need to confess?

7. What shows evidence that Nehemiah knew Scripture? (Compare 1:8 with Leviticus 26:33 and Deuteronomy 28:64; 1:10 with Deuteronomy 9:29.)

How could you use Scripture when you pray? (For examples, see Daniel 2:20-23; Jonah 2:2-9; Luke 1:46-55.)

How might you use Colossians 1:9-12 to pray for another person?

8. Of what does Nehemiah remind God? Had God been faithful in His promises to Israel? (See Joshua 21:43-45; 1 Kings 8:56.)

9. What does Nehemiah consider success?

What do the following Scriptures say about success?
- Joshua 1:6-8
- Psalm 1:1-3
- Proverbs 16:3
- Proverbs 19:8
- Proverbs 28:13

10. After studying Nehemiah 1, what do you think causes true spiritual revival in an individual or group? (See Acts 4:31 also.)

11. We all live by principles, whether good or bad, whether articulated or not. Draw one principle from Nehemiah 1 that you need to apply to your life. Turn to page 75 and write the principle on the building block #1.

LAYING THE FOUNDATION

Have you ever been so far away from home that when you received good or bad news, you felt helpless to respond or react? I recall the year I lived in Australia—a year of mixed emotions—and how the news filtered to me from home. I learned via a taped message about the untimely death of a college friend, and via a letter of the fatal heart attack of a beloved uncle. I jumped with excitement as I read in mailed newspaper clippings that the basketball team of the high school where I had taught the previous year was competing in the Indiana state finals. Some of the players had been my students. I grieved as I listened to Australia's national news one evening and the commentators broke the news of the Watergate scandal and its implications.

In each situation that brought news from home, all I could do was *pray*. In Nehemiah 1, we read about Nehemiah receiving bad news from Jerusalem, the city of his heritage. The Jews who had survived the Exile were in great trouble and disgrace. Because Jerusalem's walls lay in shambles, the rebuilt temple and the city itself were open targets for the enemies of the Jews.

We begin to see Nehemiah's potential for leadership as he not only *assessed* the needs of others, but also *ached* for them. He sat down and wept. But he didn't stop there; he fell to his knees as he *acknowledged* his need of God. For some days (actually four months), he fasted and prayed. After spending time on his knees, he *availed* himself to meet the needs he saw.

Have there been times in your life when God chose to use you to answer your own prayers? Are you willing to be used? God was going to use Nehemiah as the encourager who would see to the rebuilding of the Jerusalem walls. God often pulls us up from our knees to do what we classify as impossible. But it is on our knees that we gain the will, the wisdom, and the way. What impossible situation are you facing? Are you facing it on your knees?

As I recently wrestled with whether I should continue teaching two ladies' outreach Bible studies, I "went to my knees." Considering my health and other obligations, it was no easy decision. Yet as I was praying and reading Scripture during my quiet time one day, the Lord challenged me with Ecclesiastes 7:18: "Tackle every task that comes along, and if you fear God you can expect His blessing" (LB). He is giving the strength and the blessing!

In Nehemiah 1:5-11, Nehemiah provided a wonderful pattern for our praying. The first and most important ingredient is *praise*. Before anything else, he worshiped the Lord. Nehemiah 1:5 records, "O Lord, God of heaven, the great and awesome God, who keeps His covenant of love." When I dwell on the awesomeness of God, my troubles don't seem so awful after all.

The women I taught in the Creative Patterns Reachout decided to claim a principle as we studied Nehemiah: "Put your problems into perspective with prayer." At the conclusion of our study, my friend Nancy creatively illustrated the principle in calligraphy as a reminder. Then we printed over 200 copies for the ladies as special love gifts. I framed mine and hung it on the wall in our family room. Whenever problems envelope me, I glance at the principle and pray!

The second ingredient of Nehemiah's prayer is *penitence,* genuine sorrow for sin — so genuine that the person praying seeks to change his or her thoughts and actions. In Nehemiah 1:6-7, Nehemiah confesses the sins of the Israelites and identifies with their guilt. He prays, "We have acted very wickedly toward You. We have not obeyed the commands, decrees, and laws You gave Your servant Moses." Any unconfessed sins?

The third ingredient is *promises remembered.* Nehemiah so beautifully reminds the Lord of the promises He had already given to Israel: " 'If you are unfaithful, I will scatter you among the nations, but if you return to Me and obey My commands, then even if your exiled people are at the farthest horizon, I will gather them from there and bring them to the place I have chosen as a dwelling for My Name' " (Nehemiah 1:8-9). We frequently find that promise in the Old Testament. Of the many promises, my favorite is, "I have . . . plans to give you hope and a future. . . . You will seek Me and find Me when you seek Me with your whole heart" (see Jeremiah 29:11-14).

Be a person of promises — God's promises. He has been so faithful to show me His promises at the appropriate times of my life. I recall one specific instance when, on the night before major surgery, I anxiously clutched my Bible. After I read a few seconds where I had stopped the day before, the promise of Psalm 59:16 prevailed: "I will sing of Your strength, in the morning I will sing of Your love; for You are my fortress, my refuge in times of trouble." That promise was my "sleeping pill" that noisy night in the hospital. I faced surgery at 7:00 the next morning in His strength, not mine. As we reflect on God's promises, we gain His strength for any situation.

The last ingredient evident in Nehemiah's prayer — after praise, penitence, and promises remembered — is *petition,* the asking for God's specific help. Nehemiah prayed a measurable request. In 1:11, he asked God to give him success as he, the trusted cupbearer, approached the king. He wanted the king's sympathy and favor regarding the needs in Jerusalem. It was four months later that God provided the right time and opportunity to speak to the king.

I'm sure we could all think of times we would have acted or reacted differently had we not prayed first. Don't we often underestimate the power of prayer? One day while struggling with an emotional hurt, I reflected on the simple act of pressing the button on a garage door opener. Just as a little button lifts a door too heavy for me, so also the button of prayer allows God to lift my heavy burdens for me. "Cast all your anxiety on Him because He cares for you" (1 Peter 5:7). I prayed and His power lifted the emotional hurt.

We see Nehemiah not only gaining power but also patience through prayer. God was grooming him. The cupbearer to the king was soon to become the construction foreman for a broken-down wall. Are you praying purposefully for God's power to be released in and through you? You may not be called to build a wall in 52 days, but you are called. To what? Allow Him to show you.

ADDING REINFORCEMENT

Nehemiah was organized in his prayer life before he ever exemplified his leadership abilities. His example should challenge us to be as organized as we possibly can, especially in our prayer lives. One way to be organized is to make a *prayer list* in a notebook, where you record all the people and concerns you are praying for. You can divide it into categories, such as world and government leaders, church leaders, church events, people who need to know Christ's saving grace and power, people who are sick, friends' needs, your own personal spiritual goals and needs, and so on.

It is always encouraging to date your requests when you start praying and when the Lord answers your request. "PTL" — "Praise the Lord" — is a wonderful way to record answered prayers.

If you have children, *prayer albums* are good devices to involve them in prayer time. To make one, place pictures of people and things you are praying for in a photo album. You could even place Christmas cards you receive in an album and use it as a prayer album, praying each day for the family or individual who sent a card.

MAINTAINING DAILY UPKEEP

Just as a builder needs to check his progress daily and make sure materials, foundations, and building procedures are the best possible, we too need to check our spiritual progress and growth daily. As Nehemiah prayed in Nehemiah 1, he reminded God of His promises to Israel. Read the portions of Scripture assigned for each day and write journal entries under *Applying God's Word* on how they encourage you.

   You will be given a portion of Scripture to memorize at the start of each study as well—here, 2 Peter 1:3-4. Recite the portion each day for the remainder of the week. Entrusting God's Word to memory will build your faith firm and strong.

Day 1	Approaching God's Word:	2 Peter 1:3-4
	Applying God's Word:	
	Memorizing God's Word:	2 Peter 1:3-4
Day 2	Approaching God's Word:	Matthew 6:33
	Applying God's Word:	
Day 3	Approaching God's Word:	Matthew 28:19-20
	Applying God's Word:	
Day 4	Approaching God's Word:	1 Peter 5:6-10
	Applying God's Word:	
Day 5	Approaching God's Word:	1 Corinthians 10:13
	Applying God's Word:	
Day 6	Approaching God's Word:	Hebrews 2:14-18
	Applying God's Word:	

Day 7   Approaching God's Word: 1 John 2:23-25
           Applying God's Word:

2

PLANNING PATIENTLY

❦

GATHERING THE MATERIALS

Read Nehemiah 2:1-10.
1. Describe a time when you had to wait for something special to happen. How long did you have to wait and how patient were you?

Approximately how long did Nehemiah wait before the time was right for him to approach the king with his request?

How do we know Nehemiah was patient while waiting?

What do the following passages have to say in regard to waiting on the Lord? What are the benefits of waiting? What should we do while we wait?

❦ Psalm 27:14

❦ Psalm 40:1-4

❦ Isaiah 40:27-31

❦ 2 Corinthians 4:8-10, 16

❦ Hebrews 12:2-4

2. Read 1 Samuel 13:8-14. What happened as a result of King Saul's impatience in waiting?

3. Nehemiah 2:3 says that Nehemiah had not displayed his sorrow in front of the king before that moment. How do you think he was able to express a joyful countenance until that time?

Why, then, do you think Nehemiah showed his sorrow?

4. Why was Nehemiah afraid? (See also Ezra 4:1-23; Proverbs 16:14; Genesis 40:1-3.)

Describe a time when you were fearful. Are there any present fears you are experiencing?

Write what we should do with our fears, according to the following verses:

- ❦ 2 Samuel 22:29

- ❦ Psalm 12:7

- ❦ Psalm 27:1-3

- ❦ Psalm 46:1-2

- ❦ Psalm 56:4

- ❦ Isaiah 26:3

- ❦ Philippians 4:6-7

❦ 2 Timothy 1:7

❦ 1 Peter 5:7

5. What did Nehemiah do before he stated his request to the king, and why? (See Nehemiah 2:4.)

How does this prayer compliment the prayer of 1:5-11?

Name these Bible characters who prayed in times of great need:

Exodus 15:25 _____ 2 Kings 19:14 _____

2 Samuel 7:18 _____ 2 Chronicles 18:31 _____

1 Kings 18:37 _____

Relate a time when you shot an "arrow" prayer that God answered.

6. What was Nehemiah's initial request of the king?

How do Nehemiah's further requests demonstrate his faith?

What had he been doing during the four months he prayed?

Record what God's Word has to say in these verses about being prepared:

❦ Proverbs 16:3, 9

❦ Proverbs 20:18

❦ Proverbs 21:5

❦ Proverbs 31:13-17

❦ Luke 14:28-33

7. How much did the king provide for Nehemiah?

Did he provide more than Nehemiah asked for? (See Ephesians 3:20.)

Describe an instance when God's answer to your prayer exceeded your initial request.

8. Why do you think Nehemiah was willing to leave a comfortable position in Persia to get his hands dirty building a city wall over 800 miles away?

Can you think of another Bible character who left comfort in order to answer a call?

Does doing the Lord's will ever cause you to be uncomfortable? If so, how?

According to 1 Corinthians 15:58, why is it easy to do the Lord's work?

9. In Nehemiah 2:10, we discover the beginnings of opposition to Nehemiah's plans. What or who was the opposition, and why?

Are there any obstacles or opposition in your life spiritually? Physically? Emotionally?

What do the verses below have to say about overcoming opposition or obstacles?

❦ Deuteronomy 31:6

❦ Psalm 118:5-6

❦ Psalm 145:14

❦ Romans 8:28

❦ Romans 8:37-39

❦ Hebrews 13:5-6

10. Formulate a principle taken from Nehemiah 2:1-10 that you need to apply to your life. Turn to page 75 and write the principle on building block #2.

LAYING THE FOUNDATION

Waiting is a difficult activity to engage in at times. Perhaps you've had to wait for something special to happen—a move, a graduation, the construction of a new home or office, a wedding, or most importantly, the salvation of a loved one. The longest wait I've ever experienced was the birth of our first daughter Kim. I recall hearing her due date and thinking that it wouldn't be too long a wait. However, because of a difficult pregnancy, including hospitalization, I thought the date would never come.

One advantage of waiting is having the time to plan. It was great fun to anticipate Kim's arrival by wallpapering the nursery, making a macrame hanger (complete with ceramic teddy bears) for a swinging bassinet, buying and receiving baby items, and attending expectant parents' classes with Charles.

From the day Nehemiah received the first news of Jerusalem's plight during the month of Kislev, he not only prayed diligently but also planned deliberately. Four months later in the month of Nisan, when the time came to reveal to the king his desire to rebuild the Jerusalem wall, Nehemiah was ready. He had calculated the length of his journey, the protection necessary for it, and the amount of timber needed to rebuild the gates of the citadel by the temple, the city wall, and his residence. All these figures must have taken more than a few hours to calculate on his personal computer.

Believing that God would answer his prayers, Nehemiah planned every detail of his trip to Jerusalem. However, he waited patiently for God's timing in order to reveal his plans to the king. He allowed God to be the agent of change in the king's heart, instead of trying to manipulate the king himself. When circumstances and events don't happen as quickly as we think they should, how often we finagle until we—instead of God—are in control. I have learned that, when I take my hands off matters, God takes over and His will becomes my perfect peace.

When the time came for Nehemiah to present his requests to the king, he was "very much afraid" (2:2). Even though the prayers had been prayed and plans made, Nehemiah was still totally dependent on God for strength to face the king, for to show sadness in front of the king could have meant his death.

After Nehemiah was able to express his grief and concern for Jerusalem's predicament, the king asked, "What is it you want?" (2:4) The golden opportunity had arrived; what did Nehemiah do? He didn't rush right ahead, telling of all his wonderful plans. No, he first prayed a spontaneous prayer—an "arrow" prayer.

How many times are we guilty of relying on our own strength when God's is just a prayer away? Nehemiah knew the benefits of spontaneous prayers because we read in the Book of Nehemiah that he prayed them on at least eight occasions. He felt free to pray anytime because he had already established a personal relationship with God through deeper times of extended prayer.

In times of both blessing and burden, God desires to communicate with us more intimately than a best friend. I've often been guilty of telling good or bad news to my husband or friend first before ever talking to the Lord, who cares about every detail of my life.

I most recently discovered that God even cares about a tiny emerald on a child's birthstone ring. My parents had given a delicate ring to our daughter Kara for her Christmas present. She was proudly wearing it at our friends' large home in Lexington, Kentucky, when she announced in a panicked voice that the emerald was missing from its setting. She was heartbroken.

Knowing that we would be leaving for our home in Indiana in a few hours and that the missing emerald was a miniscule dot in a large house, I shot an arrow prayer: "Lord, You know where the emerald is; if it is Your will, please help me find it."

Though Kara had been playing all over the house with the other children, I walked first to the kitchen. There I saw a small piece of green cellophane paper wedged under the metal flooring strip between the kitchen and the back hallway. I knew it was too big to be the missing emerald, yet I knelt down to pull it out. At the time I thought it was silly to waste time picking up a piece of paper; I glanced to a spot three feet away where I saw a tiny, green speck—a sparkling emerald—just larger than a pinhead. I would never have seen it on my feet, but God had me in the right position to find it—on my knees. I shouted, "Thank You, Lord!" and Kara came happily running to see my discovery.

So often we hear that God answers prayer in three ways—yes, no, and wait. I was thinking about those answers just yesterday as I helped my husband (a pastor) during a baby dedication at the Sunday morning service. I have the fun and privilege of presenting a certificate of dedication, a carnation, and a Bible to the parents after Charles prays the dedication prayer.

When Jim and Pam Brown started to carry their four-and-a-half-month-old son James Eugene to the front of the sanctuary, I immediately started crying. I couldn't help it! Charles and our children's pastor, Bruce, began to cry too. Little James had been the subject of our church's prayers even before he was born. Learning that he would be born with a defective heart, we prayed that God would touch him with physical healing. Two days before Christmas he arrived, and God had said no to our requests.

Realizing that James would not live long without a heart transplant, we began praying for a healthy heart for him. God said to wait. Jim and Pam waited until waiting was no longer possible before God said yes, and a heart was available for James.

While Nehemiah had to wait four months, God did answer his prayer found in Nehemiah 1:5-11. However, I see that God actually answered Nehemiah's plea in a *fourth* and different way—in a way other than yes, no, or wait. God said in essence, "Nehemiah, I have a better idea—*I'll do more.*" Result: While Nehemiah had asked the king for letters of safe-conduct for his travels to Jerusalem, the king also provided him with army officers and calvary for the 800-mile trip. It meant not only protection but also a stylish arrival when he reached Jerusalem.

Ephesians 3:20-21 reminds us of God's abundant grace in answering prayers. "Now to Him who is able to do immeasurably more than all we ask or imagine, according to His power that is at work within us, to Him be glory."

Have you ever been surprised by God doing more than you requested? I have. Each year as I have made a faith pledge for missions giving during our church's missions conference, I have been amazed how God has provided all the funds through surprise means. Some years, the money that God provided was the exact amount I pledged. But most often, the Lord provided "immeasurably more" money than I had even pledged. What joy it is to be able to give the extra to missions!

I don't know why God chooses at times to do "immeasurably more." But in the meantime, I gratefully accept His provisions and watch my faith grow, preparing me for the times of testing. God must have known the opposition that would soon appear on Nehemiah's horizon, as his enemies Sanballat and Tobiah began to be disturbed with Nehemiah's zeal for the welfare of the Israelites.

Adding Reinforcement

Nehemiah's heart was in Jerusalem though he was in Babylon. As he prayed, he focused on Jerusalem. Perhaps he had a map to remind him of the "city where his fathers were buried."

Design a prayer map of your own. Buy a map of the world and, in the appropriate locations, place prayer cards of missionaries or ministries, plus pictures of friends for whom you are praying. You could also circle political or economic "hot spots" in the world which could be strategic prayer targets. What fun it could be to take a trip around the world every day on your knees!

Maintaining Daily Upkeep

Nehemiah's faith was in the God who responds to prayer. The Bible has much to say about praying in faith. Read one of the passages below each day and write a journal entry under *Applying God's Word* on how it encourages you. Memorize and recite 2 Chronicles 7:14 each day for the rest of the week.

Day 1   Approaching God's Word: 2 Chronicles 7:14
           Applying God's Word:

           Memorizing God's Word: 2 Chronicles 7:14

Day 2   Approaching God's Word: Psalm 4:3
           Applying God's Word:

Day 3   Approaching God's Word: Psalm 5:1-3
           Applying God's Word:

Day 4   Approaching God's Word: Isaiah 65:24
           Applying God's Word:

Day 5   Approaching God's Word: Luke 11:9
           Applying God's Word:

Day 6   Approaching God's Word: John 15:7
           Applying God's Word:

Day 7   Approaching God's Word: Mark 11:24; 1 John 3:21-22
           Applying God's Word:

3

PERCEIVING PROBLEMS PROPERLY

❦

GATHERING THE MATERIALS

Read Nehemiah 2:11-20.
1. Describe a time when you saw ruins from a war or natural disaster, such as a tornado, earthquake, or hurricane.

What emotions did you experience?

How do you think Nehemiah felt as he examined the broken walls of Jerusalem?

2. Why do you think Nehemiah waited three days before he inspected the walls and revealed his plans?

Why do you think he inspected the walls at night?

3. Why was Nehemiah secretive about his plans at first? Could he have used solitude for listening first to God's voice? Relate your answer to Proverbs 18:13.

What do the following Scriptures have to say about solitude?

❦ Numbers 9:8

❦ 1 Samuel 9:27

❦ 1 Kings 19:11-13

❦ Job 37:14

❦ Psalm 23:2-3

❦ Psalm 46:10

❦ Isaiah 30:15

❦ Mark 1:35

❦ Luke 5:16

How do you feel about solitude? Relate a time when solitude was a real benefit to you.

4. Find a map of Jerusalem indicating its ancient gates. Trace Nehemiah's route while inspecting the remains of the wall.

5. How did Nehemiah motivate the Jews of Jerusalem to rebuild the wall? Did he use external or internal incentives?

Describe an occasion when someone motivated you without using external rewards. How did that person do it?

Name these biblical leaders who inspired the people to follow:
❦ Exodus 12:21-28

❦ Judges 7:15-22

Can you think of others?

6. What kind of opposition did Nehemiah encounter after sharing his plan with the people? How did he respond to the opposition?

What does Nehemiah 2:19 tell us about his critics?

What causes opposition in your spiritual growth?

How do you currently respond to opposition? Read Ephesians 6:10-18 and tell how you could combat opposition.

7. How did Paul respond to opposition in 2 Corinthians 4:7-10, 16-18?

8. A good leader handles opposition well. What did King Solomon of Israel have to say in the verses below regarding leadership?

❧ Proverbs 12:24

❧ Proverbs 18:15

How did Nehemiah measure up to these Proverbs?

9. Formulate a principle from Nehemiah 2:11-20 that you need to apply to your life. Turn to page 75 and write the principle on building block #3.

LAYING THE FOUNDATION

You'll find them all over my house. They're in the windows, on the walls, on the couch, on napkin rings, in pictures, on dishes, in flowers, on my clothes, and even in my jewelry box. There's no denying it—I like butterflies! I could give many reasons why they fascinate me, but significant enough is their metamorphosis. How God changes a plain caterpillar into a beautiful butterfly is astounding. Yet He does it in the solitude of a cocoon.

It is in the solitude that the butterfly gains grace, beauty, and strength. It is in solitude too that the Lord has supplied me with His wisdom, grace, and strength. And it was in solitude that Nehemiah gained wisdom and strength to meet the challenge of rebuilding the Jerusalem wall. He *sought solitude* first of all.

After months of anticipation, prayerful waiting, careful planning, and difficult travel, Nehemiah finally arrived in Jerusalem. By that time, I'd have been more than ready to immediately start the big project and make sure everyone in Jerusalem was there to help as well. However, Nehemiah 2:11-12 records that he waited three days before telling anyone what God had put in his heart to do for the city.

What could Nehemiah have been doing those three days? I'm sure he was resting from his long trip; but more importantly, he must have been prayerfully praising and petitioning God for further guidance and wisdom for the task that confronted him. How often do you take time in solitude to re-sort your priorities and to petition the Lord for His direction concerning your life? Martin Luther once said, "I have so many things to do today that I shall spend three hours in prayer first." A spiritual leader must seek solitude to discern God's will.

Why is it that solitude is so often shunned in today's fast-paced society? Even the word *retreat,* which originally meant a place of privacy and safety has come to mean in the *Merriam-Webster Dictionary* "a period of group withdrawal for prayer, meditation, and study." People now withdraw as a group—not in solitude. I've spoken at many ladies' retreats, yet rarely have I found a woman retreating by herself to seek solitude with the Lord.

Jesus set a wonderful example of seeking solitude with His Heavenly Father. Throughout the Gospels, we catch glimpses of Him alone in the desert (see Luke 4:42), in a boat or on the mountain (see Matthew 14:13, 23-24), or in solitary places (see Mark 1:35). Luke 5:16 reads, "But Jesus often withdrew to lonely places and prayed."

Several years ago, my husband and I were sent for six weeks of ministry in the British Isles to be followed by a year of ministry in Australia. It was during my quiet time on the morning of our departure that a verse from Isaiah puzzled me. Anticipating a year of busy schedules and speaking assignments, I read, "In quietness and in confidence shall be your strength" (Isaiah 30:15b, KJV). Though I didn't know why at the time, I claimed that verse for comfort as the tears fell onto the pages of my Bible.

Though an unfamiliar verse to me, it was a well-loved one in the Commonwealth countries, as I soon realized. The first time I was asked to speak in a small group, I stood up nervously. As I faced the group, I noticed a large plaque on the back wall inscribed with "In quietness and in confidence shall be your strength." What a comfort! That verse had found its way to numerous places all over the British Isles—on paper napkins, letterheads, various plaques, mantelpieces, and plates.

On our first Sunday in Australia, a minister even included Isaiah 30:15b in his pastoral prayer. I'd like to think God arranged it all for my benefit—but probably not. It's a message we all need. However, while traveling and ministering away from family and friends, I found strength and perfect peace in His presence alone.

After seeking solitude, Nehemiah *surveyed the situation*. Nehemiah 2:12-15 records his night ride to examine the broken-down walls and destroyed gates. After developing his plan, he then dealt with the broken-down wills of the people. He *stimulated all the people* to rebuild the walls. As a skillful leader, he confronted them, saying, "You see the trouble we are in. . . . Come, let us rebuild the wall of Jerusalem, and we will no longer be in disgrace" (2:17). He also identified with the people by saying "we" and "us."

Notice that what he offered was not of material value but hard work. He didn't even offer a free trip to Hawaii to the first person who stacked 1,000 stones.

Finally, he *showed them God's faithfulness*. To see how God had provided Nehemiah with protection, direction, and provisions encouraged the people. They responded, "Let us start rebuilding" (2:18) and immediately began the good work—without one excuse.

No sooner had the work begun than the opposition began also. Nehemiah 2:19 opens with the words, "But when . . . " How is it that just about the time things start functioning smoothly, along comes some "but whens"? Some "but whens" (such as a flat tire or broken washing machine) may seem only significant enough to interrupt your plans for the day. Just the other night, I experienced a "but when" as our basement flooded shortly before our company was to sleep there and while I had a Bible study lesson to prepare. On the other hand, other "but whens" may seem awfully formidable—a move, a job change, a sickness, an adulterous mate, a loved one's death, or a cantankerous relative or neighbor.

Nehemiah's "but when" led to a complete and literal surrounding by his enemies. Yes, he had more than one enemy. Nehemiah 2:10 first introduces two of his enemies, who had received word of his arrival. At the time, Sanballat the Horonite was governor of Samaria to the north of Jerusalem; Tobiah the Ammonite was viceroy of Ammon to the east. When these men heard about Nehemiah's cause, they were very much disturbed that someone had come to promote the welfare of the Israelites. In 2:19, we read that they had recruited more trouble for the Jews in the person of Geshem the Arab, who controlled the lands to the west and south of Jerusalem. Sanballat, Tobiah, and Geshem together mocked and ridiculed Nehemiah and his supporters.

Like Nehemiah, do you ever feel surrounded—north, south, east, and west—by opposition? If you do, then like Nehemiah, you need to confront the opposition, realizing "the God of heaven will give us success" (2:20).

How often do we run away from or halfheartedly challenge the discouragement and ploys of the devil, while God wants us to realize success and victory? If we know Jesus Christ as our Savior and Lord, we must remember that "the One who is in [us] is greater than the one who is in the world" (1 John 4:4).

I too might have been tempted to ridicule Nehemiah, had I been present, for tackling such a tremendous task. Yet, I would hope that then, as now, I would have realized Nehemiah's wonderful ability to perceive problems properly through God's eyes. Proper perception comes from a proper perspective of who we are in relationship to a sovereign God who desires that we seek His wisdom to solve our problems.

ADDING REINFORCEMENT

Nehemiah gained guidance and strength from solitude. It is evident that time alone with the Lord was a high priority for him.

Try to plan a half day or even an hour that you will spend totally with the Lord. Find a special spot to be alone with your Bible, a notebook, pencil, hymnbook, and prayer list. Try to devote as much time as you can to the steps suggested below—even 30, 45, or 60 minutes *each*.

Possibilities for Prolonged Prayer

1. *Pursue God's presence*   Study the times when Jesus sought solitude with His Heavenly Father. Also examine passages that encourage us to "wait on the Lord," such as Psalms 27:14; 42:1-2; 63:1-5; Isaiah 40:31.
2. *Purify your heart*   Confess any sins that have hindered your spiritual growth. Read Psalms 32; 51; 1 John 1:9.
3. *Praise Him*   Read Psalms 103, 104, or any of the psalms listed in *Adding Reinforcement,* study 6. Write all the reasons that you should praise God. Sing or read a hymn of praise from the hymnbook.
4. *Petition Him*   Pray for the needs of others as well as your own.
5. *Plan*   Schedule daily quiet times for the next month, quarter, or year, choosing where you will read in God's Word. Make or revise your prayer lists. Set spiritual goals for yourself.

Optional Activities

1. Read a biography of a godly saint or missionary statesman.
2. Do a word study on peace, power, quietness, or waiting on the Lord.
3. Study the lives of those who developed intimate relationships with God, such as Moses, Daniel, or David.

MAINTAINING DAILY·UPKEEP

Nehemiah's faith responded to the God who understands and undergirds. Read a psalm each day; then write a journal entry under *Applying God's Word* on how that psalm might have encouraged Nehemiah regarding decisions, enemies, and problems. Record too how the psalms encourage you. Choose and write a key verse from each psalm to meditate on that day. Finally, memorize and recite Psalm 1:1-2 daily.

Day 1   Approaching God's Word: Psalm 1
          Applying God's Word:

Key verse:

Memorizing God's Word: Psalm 1:1-2

Day 2   Approaching God's Word: Psalm 25
         Applying God's Word:

Key verse:

Day 3   Approaching God's Word: Psalm 34
         Applying God's Word:

Key verse:

Day 4   Approaching God's Word: Psalm 56
         Applying God's Word:

Key verse:

Day 5   Approaching God's Word: Psalm 86
         Applying God's Word:

Key verse:

Day 6   Approaching God's Word: Psalm 142
         Applying God's Word:

Key verse:

Day 7   Approaching God's Word: Psalm 145
         Applying God's Word:

Key verse:

4

PULLING TOGETHER POWERFULLY

❧

GATHERING THE MATERIALS

Read Nehemiah 3–4.
1. Describe a time when you helped with a small part of a big project.

What kind of satisfaction did you receive? What was the end result?

Who or what motivated you?

Focus on the following select verses from Nehemiah 3–4 to identify the professions of some of the workers who were building the wall.

3:8	_____	3:17	_____
3:13	_____	3:26	_____
3:9, 15-16	_____	3:1, 28	_____
3:12	_____	3:32	_____

How do you feel about the Israelites after reading Nehemiah 3?

34

2. What do Romans 12:4-21 and Ephesians 4:2-3 have to say about (1) unity in the body of Christ, and (2) how Christians should work together?

Why are people given varying gifts? (See Ephesians 4:12-16.)

What do you think is your gift? What can you contribute to the body of Christ?

3. What do you think the triple-strand cord in Ecclesiastes 4:9-12 represents? How might you be a part of the cord?

4. What was the nature of the opposition to the building of the wall?

What was Nehemiah's immediate response to the opposition, according to Nehemiah 4:4-5, 9?

When faced with opposition, do you fight your battles on your knees?

5. Besides prayer, how could the Israelites combat opposition in these verses?

4:6 _____ 4:14 _____

4:9 _____ 4:19-23 _____

6. Have you ever become discouraged before completing a task? What things discouraged those working on the wall? (4:10-12)

Tell of someone you have known who refused to let discouragement overpower him or her.

7. Of what did Nehemiah remind the workers in 4:14, 20?
When and how did you last reflect on the greatness of God?

What do the following passages have to say regarding God's greatness?

❧ Deuteronomy 3:23

❧ 1 Chronicles 29:11-13

❧ Psalm 95:3-7

❧ Psalm 135:5

❧ Psalm 145:3-6

❧ Jeremiah 32:17-20

❧ Ephesians 1:19-20

8. Relate 2 Corinthians 4:7-10 and Romans 8:35-39 to the attitude of the Israelites.

9. Formulate a principle from Nehemiah 3–4 that you need to apply to your life. Turn to page 75 and write the principle on building block #4.

LAYING THE FOUNDATION

I just finished writing 82 thank-you notes. No, I didn't get married or have a baby. I was simply tying the loose ends from directing the drama for the Easter cantata at our church. Forty-eight of the thank-yous went to people who cut and sewed 143 costumes.

When we first thought of costuming the 120-voice choir as well as the dramatic characters, I laughed, saying, "No way!" But as we prayed and planned, everyone got excited. Choir and non-choir members alike volunteered to cut and sew. Months before the cantata, Ron and Linda Pierce began scouring every Salvation Army, Goodwill, and discount fabric store in the Indianapolis area for bargain fabric. A local business and church that had experienced smoke damage supplied old drapes having yards of usable fabric. Old sheets and curtains of various colors were toned down with donated dye.

After a cut-a-thon lasting 15 hours, the costume pieces were placed in bags for Judy Hancock to distribute to the volunteer sewers. Accessory pieces were added as costumes were sewn. Then each costume was assigned to a person according to size and role.

In my quiet time before the choir's last rehearsal, I realized the significance of Psalm 34:3: "Glorify the Lord with me; let us exalt His name together." The Easter cantata was not the effort of individuals alone but all of us working together to glorify the Lord—music composers and arrangers, choir director, choir members, actors, actresses, costume designers, sewers, sound technicians, set designers, and light technicians.

As I sat in the sound booth in the balcony during the last presentation, I cried as I realized how much the Lord was truly glorified by all of us "pulling together." There is power in pulling together when our ultimate purpose is praising God.

The Jerusalem Jews experienced that power in a far greater way as they pulled together to rebuild the wall around their city and restored temple. Nehemiah 3–4 gives us the *inspiration* as we read the list of all the people who contributed to build the wall. This passage becomes more than just a list of high priests and perfume-makers, rulers and temple servants, goldsmiths and merchants, men and women. It becomes a testimony of unity and perseverance.

Yes, perseverance—because with every inspiration comes the *inevitable*—critics who desire not only to crush spirits but defeat purposes. Perseverance is a must when confronted with critics. To be honest, I must admit that criticism is probably what defeats me most in ministry. If the devil wants me to run, he only needs to bring a critic on the scene. Lately, I've tried to listen more to the Lord than the critic. Isn't it funny how we forget all the positive effects of a ministry when one destructive criticism is aired? I remember telling our Christian Education pastor, Rick Nash, how someone else's negative criticism had bothered me. The next day he put this quote of Teddy Roosevelt's in my mailbox at church:

It is not the critic who counts. The credit actually belongs to the man in the arena, whose face is marred by dust and sweat and blood—who at best knows in the end the triumph of high achievement, and who at worst, if he fails at least fails while daring greatly, so that his place will never be with those cold and timid souls who know neither victory nor defeat" (*The Power of Commitment*, Jerry White, Colorado Springs, Colo.: NavPress, 1985, p. 100).

Critics usually resist change, breed more critics and, worst of all, forget God's power. Nehemiah's critics did all of the above, yet Nehemiah showed us how to handle criticism when Sanballat and Tobiah insulted and laughed at the Jews trying to rebuild the wall (4:1-3). These enemies said, "What are those feeble Jews doing? Will they restore their wall? Will they finish in a day? Can they bring the stones back to life from those heaps of rubble? . . . A fox . . . would break down their wall of stones!"

Nehemiah's first response to his critics was prayer (4:4). He didn't even talk to Sanballat and Tobiah at that point. So often we want to silence critics by defending ourselves. But Nehemiah turned them over to God to be silenced. Talking to God about our critics will give us peace concerning them and strength to carry on.

Another *inevitable* difficulty was discouragement. It didn't come in the beginning when enthusiasm waxed strong. Rather, discouragement crept in when the walls were halfway completed. How many times have you become discouraged halfway through a project? At the end of our sophomore year of college, my roommate and I, both burdened with financial pressures, often discussed quitting college and getting jobs. I'm glad we didn't.

If a museum were erected for unfinished projects, it would probably be the world's largest museum. In fact, I would have a few exhibits there myself. In our church's workshop/Bible study for women called Creative Patterns Reachout, we offered one workshop titled "Unfinished Projects." Participants were simply told to fellowship with one another while completing their unfinished projects. Needless to say, it was a well-populated workshop, full of honest women.

Why is it that we don't finish projects? I'm sure the number one reason would be discouragement. The discouraged Israelites said, "The strength of the laborers is giving out, and there is so much rubble that we cannot rebuild the wall" (4:10). Their enemies also threatened to kill the workers and put a stop to their work.

Through skillful leadership, Nehemiah showed the laborers how to be *invincible* not only by prayer but also by persevering and posting a guard. We read in 4:6 about the Jews persevering as they "worked with all their heart," and in 4:15-23 as they continued to build in spite of threats. Nehemiah was there to remind them that "the Lord, who is great and awesome," would fight for them (see vv. 14, 20).

Probably the most important step the Jews took was to post a guard for one another (see vv. 9, 13, 16). While half the people worked on the walls, the other half stood ready to fight the enemy.

Whether in building or supporting, each worker played an important part in the completion of the project. At times in my life, I have definitely been a "builder," right in the middle of a ministry project or spiritual growth. At other times, I have been the "supporter," standing guard for the "builders." One of the most fulfilling experiences I have had in my spiritual pilgrimage was to be a part of a prayer support group for three years with Esther, Nancy, and Cindy, three precious ladies. It was as a member of the group that I truly learned the meaning of "posting a guard."

Three of us first posted a guard by praying for Esther through the pregnancy and birth of her twin boys, Kyle and Jason. I never will forget the first time we met to share and pray after the twins were born. We joyfully passed them around as we praised the Lord for their safe arrival. I even changed a diaper. Don't ask me whose.

We posted a guard for Nancy as she faced difficulty and disappointment in trying to have a second child. She experienced one surgery during the period we prayed. Then as a second one seemed eminent, she announced her pregnancy. We happily prayed for the birth of Carly Anne.

We also had the privilege of posting a guard for each other's family members. Cindy experienced the joy of praying with her brother Bruce to receive Christ as Savior during a difficult time in his life. He has since matured and is actively ministering in his church today.

The group also prayed diligently for me as I taught the Creative Patterns Reachout Bible study and experienced all the complications from Chronic Epstein-Barr Virus Syndrome or more commonly called Chronic Fatigue Syndrome.

Like the rebuilders of the wall, I learned that we need each other to face our opposition and accomplish tasks. There is definitely power in pulling together.

ADDING REINFORCEMENT

Nehemiah 3–4 helps us realize the power possible when people pull together to accomplish a task for the Lord. Likewise, there is power when people pray together. Matthew 18:19-20 reads, "I tell you that if two of you on earth agree about anything you ask for, it will be done for you by My Father in heaven. For where two or three come together in My name, there am I with them."

Develop a prayer partnership with another Christian. Covenant to meet each week to share prayer requests and pray for one another. If you can't meet in person each week, you could pray over the telephone. (I have had a prayer partnership for 13 years and count it as one of my life's richest blessings. Can you imagine all the wonderful ways my partner and I have seen God answer prayer?)

MAINTAINING DAILY UPKEEP

Nehemiah and the Israelites gave us good examples of perseverance in spite of opposition and discouragement. Read one passage each day and write a journal entry under *Applying God's Word* about how it encourages you to persevere. Memorize and recite Galatians 6:9 daily.

Day 1   Approaching God's Word: Galatians 6:9
            Applying God's Word:

            Memorizing God's Word: Galatians 6:9

Day 2   Approaching God's Word: 1 Corinthians 9:24-27
            Applying God's Word:

Day 3   Approaching God's Word: Ephesians 6:10-20
            Applying God's Word:

Day 4   Approaching God's Word: Philippians 3:12-14
            Applying God's Word:

Day 5   Approaching God's Word: 2 Timothy 2:3-13
           Applying God's Word:

Day 6   Approaching God's Word: Hebrews 12:1-13
           Applying God's Word:

Day 7   Approaching God's Word: 1 Peter 1:14-25
           Applying God's Word:

5

PREVAILING AGAINST OPPOSITION

❧

GATHERING THE MATERIALS

Read Nehemiah 5–6.
1. How do you think the headlines on the front page of the *Jerusalem Times* might have read?

What would you consider some of the major problems in our world today? How many of these problems were prevalent among the Jews of Jerusalem? (See 5:1-5.)

2. After reading Exodus 22:25-27; Leviticus 25:35-40; and Deuteronomy 23:19-20, tell why you think Nehemiah was angry with the Jews. Did he have a right to be angry?

Describe Jesus' actions from Mark 11:15-18. Compare them to Nehemiah's actions.

In what ways did Nehemiah handle his anger wisely? (See 5:6-12.)

How did he confront the Jews? What were the results?

3. What do the following passages have to say about helping and reacting to those in need?

❦ Deuteronomy 15:4-11

❦ Proverbs 14:21, 31

❦ Proverbs 22:22

❦ Proverbs 31:9, 20

❦ Matthew 6:2-4

4. What warnings do the following verses make about greed?

❦ Proverbs 15:27

❦ Luke 12:15

❦ Ephesians 5:5

❦ James 4:1-3

❦ 1 Peter 5:2

5. Describe a time when you observed someone sacrificially giving so that someone else less fortunate could have?

How did Nehemiah sacrificially give while he was governor at Jerusalem? (See 5:14-18.)

How did his actions reflect the point of 1 Corinthians 12:26?

Record from these verses how Jesus sacrificially gave for us:

❦ John 12:23-26

❦ Hebrews 7:27

❦ Hebrews 9:15, 26-28

❦ 1 John 1:7

Have you given sacrificially for someone less fortunate?

6. After Nehemiah handled the internal strife in Nehemiah 5, he was hit head-on with external pressure and opposition. What was the pressure in 6:1-4? What plans did his enemies lay to trap him?

7. How was Nehemiah slandered in 6:5-7? How did he react to the accusation?

   According to Proverbs 10:18 and 11:9, how can slander harm? How did David pray in Psalm 7 regarding his being slandered?

   How do you react when someone has slandered you?

8. How had Tobiah tried to threaten Nehemiah? (See 6:17-19.)

9. How did Nehemiah handle the temptation in 6:10-14?

   How do you handle temptation?

   What do the following Scriptures say regarding temptation?
   ❦ 1 Corinthians 10:13

   ❦ 1 Timothy 6:11-12

   ❦ 2 Timothy 2:22

   ❦ James 1:12-15

   ❦ 2 Peter 2:9

10. Describe a time when you didn't think a project could ever be finished; yet, with the Lord's miraculous intervention, it was.

What happens when we are dependent on the Lord?

How did the Jews' enemies react when the wall was completed in 52 days? (See 6:15-16.)

11. Formulate a principle from Nehemiah 5–6 that you need to apply to your life. Turn to page 75 and write the principle on building block #5.

LAYING THE FOUNDATION

One only needs to read Nehemiah 5:1-5 to realize the reality of the saying, "There's nothing new under the sun." Compare some headlines from the *Jerusalem Journal* (written at the start of *Gathering the Materials*) with those in today's *Wall Street Journal* or *USA Today*. Some common headlines might be: "Interest Rates Soar," "Drought Causes Crop Failures," "Famine Spreads," "Workers Call Strike," "Public Outcry Over Tax Increases," or "City on Brink of Bankruptcy." Sound familiar, don't they? At this point in the story, one wonders if the Jerusalem wall would ever be completed.

In spite of two debilitating kinds of opposition—internal strife and external schemes—the Jerusalem Jews prevailed and completed the wall in 52 days. Let's see how they did it under Nehemiah's confrontational leadership.

First of all, Nehemiah confronted the rich taking advantage of the poor. Nehemiah 5:1-13 records the dissatisfaction of the poor as a direct result of the disobedience of the rich. The poor were protesting and wanting to stop work on the wall literally to survive. The richer Jews who had become wealthy either in exile or through inheritance were charging high interest on loans. When the people couldn't repay the loans, the rich would confiscate their property. With no means of income the poor would then be forced to sell their children into slavery.

Realizing the situation, Nehemiah became angry. At that point he began to deal with the disobedience of the rich. In confronting their sinfulness, he reminded them of God's laws regarding charging interest (see Exodus 22:25-27; Leviticus 25:35-40; Deuteronomy 23:19-20). God had clearly said they were not to charge a fellow Jew interest or to hold his cloak as a pledge past sunset. If we want to check for disobedience in any area of our own lives, we best measure ourselves against God's Word as our standard; for it is perfect and leads to conviction (see Psalm 19:7-11; Hebrews 4:12).

As I read the Bible each day, God often uses His Word to convict me of sin in my life. I recall a cold, snowy January 12 when I piously sat at my kitchen table for my morning quiet time. I could hear the faint whimpers of a little black poodle puppy I had locked in the laundry room a few feet away. At that point in history—his and mine—I couldn't stand that puppy. In fact, it might be more honest to say I hated him.

However, it had been a "love turned to hate" relationship. Only two months earlier when my husband returned from visiting a new family in our church, he announced that he had purchased a Christmas present for our two-year-old daughter Kim—the newborn black poodle he had held in his hand. Assuring me that the dog would be weaned and completely housebroken by Christmas, he said he would pick up the puppy on Christmas morning. What a delight to watch Kim's face as she opened the box to find the cute, little black poodle with a red bow! They quickly became friends and he began to follow her around like a shadow, thus earning the name "Shadow." I thought he was darling too—that is, for about an hour, until I discovered he wasn't housebroken.

By January 12, I had tried every trick I had heard or read about to train Shadow, with no success. Being several months pregnant, I was growing weary of cleaning up his messes. So I did the only thing a person could do: I permanently displaced him. No matter how loudly he yelped, I yelled back, "No way, Shadow!" That continued until I read Proverbs 12:10, "A righteous man cares for the needs of his animal."

Needless to say, I certainly didn't feel very righteous after reading those convicting words. I had to ask the Lord for a right attitude, even a loving attitude, toward Shadow. I prayed, "Lord, if You want me to love Shadow, You're going to have to love him through me." God was faithful, and Shadow and I became good friends.

Fortunately, the Israelites were quick to respond to God's Word (see Nehemiah 5:12-13). However, there are times when we are slow to respond or want to forget His discipline altogether. I'm reminded of a time when my daughter gave an adultlike response at age three. I had told her that I would have to unhappily pull the car off the road and spank her with the little wooden spoon if she continued to spread the chewing gum from one side of the back seat to the other. When I said how I didn't like to use the spoon, she quickly replied, "Mommy, if you don't like that spoon either, why don't we just throw it out the window?" Meanwhile, we believers say, "God, why don't we just forget about the discipline and the consequences?"

After Nehemiah confronted the internal strife, he began to experience the external schemes of Sanballat, Tobiah, Geshem, and the rest of his enemies. Since the wall was almost restored and the doors of the gates ready to be hung, the enemies desperately tried four different plots to stop the completion.

The first plot (6:1-4) was the *distraction* plot, when Nehemiah's enemies invited him four times to meet them in the plain of Ono, a verdant, restful place. It would have been a nice break for Nehemiah had he not discerned their desire to kill him. When the devil tempts us to retreat to the "plain of Ono" (a place in our lives that would hinder our spiritual progress), we should say, "Oh, no!"

Second came the *defamation* plot (vv. 5-9) when the enemies accused the Jews in an open letter of planning a rebellion, and Nehemiah of trying to overthrow the king. Nehemiah again confronted his enemies' lies, and most important of all, he prayed: "Now strengthen my hands" (6:9). When your character is attacked, do you pray for strength, rather than counterattacking?

The third plot was the *disobedience* plot (vv. 10-13). Tobiah hired the false prophet Shemaiah to "prophesy" that men were coming at night to kill Nehemiah, and to suggest he (Nehemiah) should hide in the temple. For Nehemiah, who was not a priest, to hide in the temple would have been a direct disobedience of God's Law. The discerning Nehemiah refused the suggestion and prayed that the Lord would take proper revenge on his enemies (v. 14). When is the last time you completely turned your enemies over to the Lord?

The fourth plot Tobiah tried in order to stop Nehemiah was the *discouragement* plot (vv. 17-19). Because Tobiah had relatives in Jerusalem, he had an inside track both to find out progress on the wall and strengthen his own support. He sent letters to his family to intimidate, and to discourage, Nehemiah.

In spite of all the opposition, the wall was completed in an astounding 52 days. Even the enemies "were afraid and lost their self-confidence, because they realized that this work had been done with the help of our God" (v. 16).

Are there times when you feel like the opposition is just too great? It may come at you disguised as distraction, defamation, temptation to disobedience, or discouragement. But God wants us to prevail—finish His project—in our lives. He wants us all to mature (see Heb. 6:1) and to escape temptation (see 1 Cor. 10:13). He wants us to realize that "the One who is in [us] is greater than the one who is in the world" (1 John 4:4).

ADDING REINFORCEMENT

Nehemiah 5–6 demonstrates how to truly prevail against opposition by "posting a guard" for one another. A great way to do so is to form a prayer support group of four people who will meet each week or every other week. During the meeting time, tell each other how you can most effectively pray for one another, especially in the areas of weaknesses. You can hold each other accountable for spiritual growth and share with each other what the Lord is teaching you through your daily quiet times. The personal goals of your partners can become matters of prayer as well.

MAINTAINING DAILY UPKEEP

Nehemiah and the Jews were faced with a seemingly impossible task and surrounded by all kinds of opposition. Yet Nehemiah knew the God who fights all our battles. Perhaps you are facing battles of your own. Read the passage for each day and write a journal entry under *Applying God's Word* on how you will depend on the Lord. If the passage of the day is a psalm, find and record a key verse. Memorize 1 John 4:4 and recite it daily through the week.

Day 1   Approaching God's Word: Exodus 14:13-14; 2 Chronicles 16:9; 1 John 4:4

          Applying God's Word:

          Memorizing God's Word: 1 John 4:4

Day 2   Approaching God's Word: Psalm 17
          Applying God's Word:

          Key verse:

Day 3   Approaching God's Word: Psalm 31
          Applying God's Word:

          Key verse:

Day 4   Approaching God's Word: Psalm 35
          Applying God's Word:

          Key verse:

Day 5   Approaching God's Word: Psalm 57
          Applying God's Word:

Key verse:

Day 6   Approaching God's Word: Psalm 59
         Applying God's Word:

         Key verse:

Day 7   Approaching God's Word: John 16:33; Romans 8:35-
                                    37
         Applying God's Word:

         Key verse:

6

PUTTING A PRIORITY ON GOD'S WORD

❦

GATHERING THE MATERIALS

Read Nehemiah 8–9.

1. When is the last time you stood or sat still for an event that lasted approximately six hours?

   What held the Israelites' attention for a similar period of time?

   How did Ezra guide them? (See 8:1-6.)

2. What was the attitude of the people toward God and His Word?

   What is your attitude toward God and His Word?

   What do the following verses say our attitude should be?
   - ❦ Job 23:12

   - ❦ Psalm 42:1-2

   - ❦ Psalm 63:1

   - ❦ Psalm 77:2

   - ❦ Psalm 143:5-6

   - ❦ Isaiah 26:9

   - ❦ 1 Peter 2:1-3

Why is understanding God's Word important? How were the people helped to understand? (See 8:2-3, 7-8, 12.)

3. How did the people respond to the reading of God's Word? (See vv. 3, 5-6, 9.) Why do you think they responded in these ways?

Why did Nehemiah say, "The joy of the Lord is your strength"? (v. 10) Why, then, could the people celebrate with joy?

4. What happened on the second day of the month? (See v. 13ff.) What did the Jews discover regarding how they should celebrate? (See 8:14-18.) Why were they to celebrate in this way? (See Leviticus 23:34-36.) How did they respond to the command?

What do these passages have to say about obedience?
   ❦ 1 Samuel 15:22-23

   ❦ John 14:21

   ❦ John 15:10

   ❦ Acts 5:29

   ❦ Romans 6:16-18

5. What happened as a result of the Israelites' obedience? (See 9:1-3.)

When is repentance genuine, according to 2 Chronicles 7:14, Ezra 10:1, and Luke 18:13?

6. Read the prayer of 9:5-37. What was the people's overall attitude toward God? (See v. 33.)

Challenge: Write a prayer modeled loosely after 9:5-37 which portrays your spiritual pilgrimage with God.

Are there similarities to the prayer of the Israelites?

7. What are some consequences of disobedience, as revealed in verses 26-27 and 33-37?

Who disobeyed God in these passages?

❦ Numbers 20:8-12

❦ 1 Samuel 15:3, 8-9, 16-36

❦ Numbers 4:15; 2 Samuel 6:6-7

❦ Jeremiah 7:21-29

8. How did the Israelites make a recommitment to God?

What does God's Word say is promised to those with penitent hearts?

❦ Psalm 34:18

❦ Psalm 51:17

❦ Isaiah 66:2

❦ 2 Corinthians 7:10

9. Formulate a principle from Nehemiah 8–9 that you need to apply to your life. Turn to page 75 and write the principle on building block #6.

LAYING THE FOUNDATION

As I sit on my back porch, I smell the fresh air, hear the birds singing praises to their Maker, and watch the columbine, iris, roses, and peonies open their delicate petals. It's spring! Revival is in the air! Just two months ago, I could only glance out the back porch door to observe a cold, bleak landscape—no flowers, no grass, no blue sky, and no birds. Yet God in His wondrous power has brought it all to life again. He has revived my backyard with His sunshine and warmth.

Just as the ingredients of sunshine and warmth need to be present for the revival of my backyard each spring, there need to be certain ingredients present for spiritual revival. In Nehemiah 8–9, we observe these ingredients in the hearts and lives of the Israelites, who demonstrated *receptivity, repentance, responsiveness,* and *rejoicing.*

Most important was the Israelites' *receptivity* to God's Word. They had requested Ezra, the priest, to read from the Law of God which had been given to Moses. The people literally stood and listened for hours from morning until noon (see 8:1-5). In today's society, it takes a fast-moving championship ball game, a tension-filled movie, or an earthshaking news event to hold our attention for any length of time. During the Gulf Crisis in early 1991, we heard of people who watched television 24 hours a day. Even then, though, I'm sure they also sat down to watch the news. But the Israelites were so hungry to hear God's Word, they stood attentively day after day for hours.

So often we give such feeble excuses for not reading a small portion of God's Word each day. When is the last time you asked the Lord to give you a hunger and thirst for His Word? (See Psalms 42:1-2; 63:1-3.) How receptive is your heart?

When discipling women, I often have heard the honest response, "But I just don't have the desire to make it a priority to read and study the Bible. How can I then have a consistent quiet time?"

I'll agree with these women that desire is important. That's why I always direct their attention to Philippians 2:13, "For it is God who works in you to will and to act according to His good purpose." God gives not only the desire but also the ability to do His will. I have found that doing God's will helps us gain greater desire for it. Connoisseurs of special delicacies don't train their taste buds instantly.

If a living thing is to grow, it must be fed and watered—it's a simple fact. If a person is to grow spiritually, she must feed on God's Word.

Since the Israelites had not heard God's Word during the 70 years of their exile in Babylon, they were very hungry to hear what it had to say. They were so hungry to understand too that the Levites circulated among them and "instructed the people in the Law while the people were standing there . . . making it clear and giving the meaning so that the people could understand what was being read" (Nehemiah 8:7-8).

Once they heard the Word, the people showed *repentance* for their sins and disobedience, weeping openly with remorse. But Ezra reminded them that "the joy of the Lord is your strength" (v. 10) and that they should celebrate because they could hear and understand God's Word. At a later time when they heard the Word, they spent several hours confessing their sins (9:1-3).

After the celebration recorded in Nehemiah 8:10-12, the people came together for further reading and guidance from the Word. When they heard about God's command to remember His faithfulness to the Israelites during their journey from Egyptian exile to the Promised Land, they built booths (tents or huts) for their families and celebrated the seven-day Feast of Tabernacles (see Leviticus 23:33-43).

Because the Jews had put God's Word first in their lives, they demonstrated *responsiveness* to His commands. Likewise, when we are growing in the Lord and striving to be holy, it is easier to be responsive and submissive to His will. John 14:15 records Jesus' words, "If you love Me, you will obey what I command."

Jesus also taught us how to be obedient. He said, "But the world must learn that I love the Father and that I do exactly what My Father has commanded Me" (John 14:31). Philippians 2:8 reads, "He humbled Himself and became obedient to death—even the death on a cross!" If God loves me that much, my only response can be love and obedience in return.

I have discovered that obedience is easier when I'm asked "to do" than when I'm asked "to be." Why is this so? Attitudes seem to be where the devil often gets his first victories. The Apostle Paul must have understood this because many of his epistles deal with attitudes.

One attitude that was obvious among the Israelites was *rejoicing.* Several times we read of their very great joy (see 8:10, 12, 17; 9:4-5). What a tremendous period of celebration! When sins are confessed and a heart is right with God, the face is the first to know. Then the tongue knows, because praise becomes a prominent part of the vocabulary. I watched a 69-year-old lady, Edna McKeel (great grandmother of little James Eugene from chapter 2), be baptized after accepting Christ at the conclusion of a Sunday service two weeks before. Her family had prayed for her salvation for over 30 years. As she came out of the water, she smiled and said, "Oh, how I love God!"

The Israelites spent much time praising God. I especially like the instructions of the Levites, "Stand up and praise the Lord your God, for He lives from everlasting to everlasting. Praise His glorious name! It is far greater than we can think or say" (9:5, LB). The rest of Nehemiah 9 is a prayer of praise remembering all that God had done for the nation of Israel in spite of their disobedience.

When is the last time you took time to truly praise the Lord? Have you developed an attitude of praise that pervades your being? Or have you begun to take God for granted?

One of my favorite syndicated cartoons is "The Family Circus" by Bill Keane. I have saved one cartoon from several years ago where, in the first frame, the mother is joyfully thinking of all her blessings. The second frame shows her hugging her husband and saying how fortunate they are. In the third frame, she is praying and thanking God for everything. I chuckle as I read the last frame which shows what happens in heaven when the mother's praise is received. A bell is rung, the choir sings the "Hallelujah Chorus," and angels respond with, "Hey! Didja hear that? She didn't ask for a thing! God's well-pleased. It's hard to believe—no request! This is one for the books. Way to go, down there!"

Though the cartoon is humorous, it is also convicting because our prayers often contain more of our petitions than the praise which God desires. "Through Jesus, therefore, let us continually offer to God a sacrifice of praise—the fruit of lips that confess His name" (Hebrews 13:15). "How good it is to sing praises to our God, how pleasant and fitting to praise Him!" (Psalm 147:1-2)

The Israelites realized that there was power for revival when they put a priority on God's Word, repented for their sins, responded in obedience, and praised Him. Do you want to experience God's presence? Then praise Him! "God inhabits the praise of His people" (Psalm 22:3).

ADDING REINFORCEMENT

The Israelites experienced true spiritual revival as they put a priority on reading God's Word and praising Him. Why not combine the two by praying through some of the psalms? The following is a list of psalms that are full of praise to God: Psalms 8–9; 18–19; 29; 33–34; 46–48; 63; 66; 89; 92–93; 95–96; 98; 100; 103–105; 108; 111; 113; 117; 134–136; 139; 145–150. Read these psalms as if they were your own prayers of praise to God. When you do so, try to answer the following questions: **Who should offer praise? To whom should we offer praise? Why are we to praise? How are we to praise? When are we to praise? Where are we to praise?**

Psalm 103 is a wonderful model of a psalm of praise. Write your own poem of praise to the Lord, following this model.

Commit to praise God every day!

MAINTAINING DAILY UPKEEP

After Nehemiah rebuilt the wall, he knew the ultimate priority was to reform the Jews spiritually. So he delegated the challenge to Ezra the priest, who focused the people's attention on what speaks best— God's Word. Psalm 119 is a beautiful psalm about God's Word and its importance. Some say it was actually written by Ezra after the temple had been rebuilt (Ezra 6:14-15) as a repetitive meditation on God's Word, its beauty, and its challenge. Read Psalm 119 this week and apply how its principles challenge you to study God's Word more diligently. Memorize and recite Psalm 119:1-2 daily.

Day 1   Approaching God's Word: Psalm 119:1-24
           Applying God's Word:

           Memorizing God's Word: Psalm 119:1-2

Day 2   Approaching God's Word: Psalm 119:25-48
         Applying God's Word:

Day 3   Approaching God's Word: Psalm 119:49-80
         Applying God's Word:

Day 4   Approaching God's Word: Psalm 119:81-104
         Applying God's Word:

Day 5   Approaching God's Word: Psalm 119:105-128
         Applying God's Word:

Day 6   Approaching God's Word: Psalm 119:129-152
         Applying God's Word:

Day 7   Approaching God's Word: Psalm 119:151-176
         Applying God's Word:

7

PROMISING OBEDIENCE PENITENTLY

❦

GATHERING THE MATERIALS

Read Nehemiah 10–11.
1. Describe a time you placed your signature on an agreement.

As you glance over the names of the Israelites who signed the binding agreement with God, what impresses you most?

2. What was the overall commitment of the Israelites to God? (See 10:29.) Why do you think they wanted to put it in writing?

3. Name specific ways from verses 30-39 in which the Jews agreed to obey God.

4. God has reasons for His laws. According to Exodus 34:12-16 and Deuteronomy 7:1-4, why did God not want the Jews to intermarry with other peoples?

What happened in the life of King Solomon as a result of his disobedience to this command? (See 1 Kings 11:1-13.)

Compare the principle you learn to that of 2 Corinthians 6:14–7:1. Are there things or people which hinder your devotion to God? What occupies your thoughts and energy?

What do we need to do, according to Matthew 6:24; Romans 12:1-2; and 1 John 2:15?

Do you think God wants Christians to completely avoid non-Christians? What does He really desire for us in our relationships with them? (See Matthew 5:13-16; Luke 5:27-32; 1 Corinthians 5:9-10; 7:12-13.)

5. Why did God want the Sabbath Day to be sacred? (See Exodus 20:8-11; Deuteronomy 5:12-15.)

As Christians, we consider Sunday our Sabbath day because it was Jesus' day of resurrection. How do you regard Sunday? Is it a day of rest?

6. Why did God establish a Sabbath year? (See Exodus 23:11; Leviticus 25:4-7.)

Our first question would probably be: "Well, wouldn't the people all starve?" But God always provides for our obedience. Explain from Leviticus 25:20-22 how God provided for the Jews when they obeyed.

7. God did not want His temple or the worship in it neglected. How did He provide for their needs to be met? (See Nehemiah 10:32-39.)

Why is it important that God be given the "firstfruits"? (See Exodus 13:1-2; Numbers 3:40-51.)

8. Many were eager to see Jerusalem restored as the capital and holy city. According to Nehemiah 11:1-2, how was Jerusalem to be repopulated?

Why do you think people were hesitant to move to Jerusalem?

9. As you read in Nehemiah 11 the composition of Jerusalem's new citizenry, what variety of jobs do you observe?

Just as Jerusalem consisted of important individuals with unique jobs, so the church body consists of individuals who "pull together" in unity. According to 1 Corinthians 12:12-31, describe the importance of each part in the whole body reaching a common goal.

What do you think you are contributing to the body of Christ? What part of the body would you consider yourself to be? (See Romans 12:6-8.)

10. Formulate a principle from Nehemiah 10–11 that you need to apply to your life. Turn to page 75 and write the principle on building block #7.

LAYING THE FOUNDATION

On June 4, 1971, I made an extremely important agreement. It wasn't walking down the aisle, saying the vows, exchanging rings, or even kissing my new husband that made the agreement legal. Our marriage was recognized by the state of Indiana when, in front of witnesses, I signed "Vicki Lynn Richards" on the marriage license.

In August 1983, my husband and I made another major agreement. It wasn't seeing the "For Sale" sign in the front yard at 539 Lazy Lane, viewing the inside of the house, dreaming about the future ministry with people in the home, securing finances, or moving in our furniture that made the home legally ours. It was made legally ours when, in front of witnesses, we signed on the dotted lines.

Placing one's signature on a document signifies that you are serious about your decision. Nehemiah 10 contains a list of men who signed a covenant with God on behalf of the entire Jewish nation. They were serious in their agreement with God in 9:38. Their seriousness had resulted from genuine repentance and confession. When people are truly repentant for their sins, they will turn from their sinful ways and make every effort, with God's help, to change.

Of course, changing is more drastic for some people than for others. I recently sat in a hotel room at a ladies' retreat listening to a young woman who had given her life to Christ. Due to her past sins, she was still dealing with some emotional problems; still, it was evident that Christ had drastically transformed her life. She had been deeply involved with witchcraft and devil worship before she had experienced the freedom of Christ's forgiveness and liberation from sinful bondage. As she tearfully described some of the horrible deeds from her past, I lovingly reminded her that God's eraser is the best because Christ paid for those sins with His shed blood. He forgives and forgets! (See Hebrews 10:17-18.)

The Israelites had literally spent days confessing their sins. In conclusion, they wanted to declare their obedience to God with four important promises.

First of all, the Israelites agreed not to intermarry with other peoples (see Nehemiah 10:30). They had been warned by God for generations to not intermarry because it would lead to the worship of foreign gods (see Deuteronomy 7:1-4). Let's face it. God is a jealous God, and rightfully so; He wants no divided loyalties (see Matthew 6:24).

Second, the people agreed to keep the Sabbath Day holy (see Nehemiah 10:31). One of the Ten Commandments that God gave the Israelites while they were encamped at Mt. Sinai on their way to the Promised Land was to "Remember the Sabbath Day by keeping it holy" (Exodus 20:8). On the Sabbath Day, they were not to work but to rest and worship God. The Jerusalem Jews, for this reason, forbade trade on that day. At that point in time, because obedience was more important than wealth, the Jews did not compromise their values.

Third, the Jews agreed to keep the Sabbath year (see Nehemiah 10:31), which meant that they were to let the soil rest from crops every seventh year (see Leviticus 25:4-7). Now, if I had been an Israelite, this law would have been the hardest for me to obey because it took an act of faith that the sixth year's crop would provide enough until the eighth year's crop was harvested. Yet God promised His reward for obedience in Leviticus 25:20-22: "I will send you such a blessing in the sixth year that the land will yield enough for three years."

Fourth, the Jews agreed to care for the temple and worship needs (see Nehemiah 10:32-39). They would pay a temple tax to care for the temple and worship supplies. They would supply wood for the burnt offerings as well as the firstfruits of their crop yields. They also promised to bring a tenth of their produce for tithes.

As a child, I was happiest when I was obedient and submissive to my parents and those in authority over me. However, I remember very distinctly one time when I disobeyed the rules. My girlfriend and I had pedaled our bicycles to a park about two miles from our homes to play tennis on the new tennis courts. I couldn't wait to get there. For days I had envisioned myself strutting onto those courts as if I were a Wimbledon champion.

As we approached the courts, we noticed that the gates were closed. Closer observance told us they were padlocked. No one was around, including the park superintendent, so we decided to help ourselves to the courts by shinnying up the 14-foot-high fence. I giggled with every foot covered until I reached the top of the fence. Then I froze! No matter how much coaxing my friend gave I couldn't budge one inch. Perched like a bird on a high wire, I began to shake nervously until the whole fence was reverberating and rattling. I thought for sure the park superintendent would hear. Disobedience to the rules combined with a newly formed fear of heights to create a seemingly impossible situation.

My friend finally took my feet, one at a time, and moved them slowly down the fence until I was securely on the ground. Needless to say, I haven't climbed a fence since that day.

Unlike me on top of the fence, the Israelites experienced peace and joy as a result of their obedience to their promises. Nehemiah 11–12 tells of the Israelites' 12 years of obedience. Nehemiah had been in Jerusalem that long before he returned to King Artaxerxes in Babylon, though it had taken only 52 days to complete the wall.

When people obey God, they not only experience peace but exemplify submission. The Israelites were willing to repopulate Jerusalem by moving back into the city. Some volunteered and others moved gladly as they were selected (11:1-3). Many served in various ways by working within the temple (vv. 10-12), working outside the temple (vv. 15-16), leading prayer services (v. 17), singing at the temple (v. 23), and assisting in all matters of public administration (v. 24).

There is such an emphasis on power in today's society. We hear of power summit, power money, power tools, power ties, power plays, and the power of positive thinking. I recently saw an advertisement for Fantastik cleaner that said, "More power for more places." The November 1990 *Ladies Home Journal* dedicated its whole issue to the topic "Never Underestimate the Power of a Woman," featuring America's fifty most powerful women and concluding with an article entitled, "50 Ways to Use Your Power." Yet, I venture to say that none of these kinds of power can even compare with the power displayed by the obedient Israelites. They "pulled together" not only to rebuild Jerusalem's walls in 52 days but also to repopulate and reestablish the city as the center of worship to the all-powerful God. One can truly never underestimate the power available when God's people pray, obey, and "pull together."

ADDING REINFORCEMENT

There were many Israelites who signed the agreement with God in Nehemiah 10. They were making a public commitment to Him by their involvement and signatures. One way to get many people involved in a strategic prayer concern is to form an organized prayer chain. Your prayer chain could consist of people committed to praying and to following some simple rules, such as our church's prayer chain has used for several years.

When you pass along a request:
1. Consider whether or not the situation is serious enough to involve all who are in the prayer ministry.
2. Make sure you have the correct information.
3. Write the need or request in one or two concise sentences which can be clearly and easily passed on.
4. Call the first person in the chain between 8:00 and 9:00 A.M. or 6:00 and 7:00 P.M. An emergency request can be called at any time.
5. Share answers to prayer. If you have involved the prayer chain members in prayer, they have the right to know the outcome.

When you receive a request:
1. Take time to write down the request so you can clearly pass it

on. Keep the request on your prayer list.
2. Call the next person on the chain. If you can't reach her, continue down the chain until you reach someone. Call the persons you missed later.
3. Pray as soon as you can by yourself or with your family.

MAINTAINING DAILY UPKEEP

No matter what part of the body of Christ we are, God wants us to serve Him with right attitudes. Read and apply the following passages to ascertain how you should serve. Memorize and recite Matthew 23:11-12 daily.

Day 1   Approaching God's Word: Matthew 23:11-12
        Applying God's Word:

        Memorizing God's Word: Matthew 23:11-12

Day 2   Approaching God's Word: Deuteronomy 10:12-13; Psalm 2:11
        Applying God's Word:

Day 3   Approaching God's Word: Matthew 5:3-12; 6:24
        Applying God's Word:

Day 4   Approaching God's Word: Galatians 5:13-14; Ephesians 6:7-8
        Applying God's Word:

Day 5   Approaching God's Word: Philippians 2:1-8
        Applying God's Word:

Day 6   Approaching God's Word: 1 Peter 3:3-5

Applying God's Word:

Day 7 Approaching God's Word: 1 Peter 4:7-11
Applying God's Word:

8

PURIFYING OURSELVES
FOR SERVICE

❦

GATHERING THE MATERIALS

Read Nehemiah 12–13.
1. Nehemiah 12 is a chapter of intense celebration to dedicate the Jerusalem wall. Who came together for the dedication?

2. Before the celebration began, the Levites and priests first ceremonially purified themselves, the people, and the wall. What do you think "purify" means?

When and why was the purification process necessary? (See 2 Chronicles 29:3-11.) What did King Hezekiah summon the priests and Levites to do?

After the purification process, what did Hezekiah do? (See 2 Chronicles 29:15-19.)

3. Throughout the Old Testament, sacrifice was the way that man could atone for his sins and restore a right relationship with God. The animal sacrifice did two things: (1) the animal symbolically paid for sin's penalty, and (2) the animal's death represented one life given for another. According to Hebrews 10:1-14, why do we no longer need to make animal sacrifices?

Have you accepted Christ as the sacrifice for your sins? If not, read John 3:16; Romans 5:8; and 10:9-13. Confess your sins, ask Him to forgive you, and believe in Him.

4. Recall a time when someone broke a promise to you. How did you feel? Having been in Jerusalem 12 years, Nehemiah returned to Babylon. After an unspecified period of time, he traveled again to Jerusalem, only to experience a heartache common to those in leadership. What did Nehemiah discover, according to these passages?

   ❦ 13:7-9, 23-31

   ❦ 13:10-14

   ❦ 13:15-22

   How did Nehemiah confront the people?

5. How do you think God felt when the Jews broke every promise they had made to Him?

   Why do you think they did?

   Have you ever promised something to God and not followed through?

6. How did the Jews respond to Nehemiah's confrontations and reforms?

   What lessons can we learn from Nehemiah's confrontation to deal with disobedience in our lives?

7. In what three ways did Nehemiah ask God to remember him?

How do you want to be remembered?

8. Formulate a principle from Nehemiah 12–13 that you can apply to your life. Turn to page 75 and write the principle on building block #8.

LAYING THE FOUNDATION

The adage "While the cat's away, the mice will play" always made me chuckle—that is, until this year. Having been a middle school and high school English teacher before our children were born, I thought it would be fun to do some substitute teaching this year. I have enjoyed the experience—yes, even junior high band and physical education classes. However, I quickly discovered that I would much rather be the classroom teacher than the substitute. I could probably write a book on everything students told me their classroom teachers supposedly let them do. One student even told me that the teacher let the class go to lunch 15 minutes early every day. Now do you think I really believed all their antics and excuses? Not for a minute. Because I had been a teacher, I knew better.

Nehemiah must not have had a very good substitute when he returned to Babylon 12 years after he had arrived in Jerusalem. We don't know how long Nehemiah was gone but it was long enough for the Israelites to have completely broken three specific promises they had made to God in Nehemiah 10–11. Lack of time probably kept them from breaking the fourth.

First of all, the Jews had neglected the temple (see 13:1-14). They had not given their tithes to help support the Levites and singers, who were forced to go back to their fields for livelihood (v. 10). Eliashib, the priest, had even allowed Tobiah, Nehemiah's enemy, to occupy a large room in the temple, which formerly held grain offerings, tithes, and temple articles. Eliashib had also married Tobiah's daughter.

Often when sin is allowed into our lives little by little, it takes up permanent residence. Then our bodies, which are the Lord's temple (see 1 Corinthians 6:19-20) become defiled. At one time or another, we've all watched sadly as a friend or loved one gradually compromised with sin until it took hold and destroyed his or her Christian witness. Whole churches have been seriously affected by one person's sin. Satan desires to devour and destroy (see 1 Peter 5:8).

Second, the people had neglected the Sabbath (see Nehemiah 13:15-22). They were working on the Sabbath as well as buying and selling.

Third, the Israelites had intermarried with women from Asdod, Ammon, and Moab. Half of their children did not even know the language of the Jews.

Nehemiah must have been heartbroken as he saw the deplorable way the people were living. As he looked around, he probably recalled the glorious time in the history of Jerusalem when the people had celebrated and dedicated the wall, as recorded in Nehemiah 12. The priests and Levites had first purified themselves, the people, and the wall (see 12:30). Then they were a nation clean and pure before God, ready to consecrate themselves to His service. Now they had become condemned and putrid in His sight because of their disobedience. No matter how depraved the sin or situation, however, God is ready and willing to cleanse and purify repentant hearts (see 1 John 1:9).

Nehemiah's leadership abilities proved just as great when confronting the people with their waywardness as when challenging them to rebuild the wall. First of all, he *rebuked* them for every broken promise. He asked, "Why is the house of God neglected?" (13:11) "What is this wicked thing you are doing—desecrating the Sabbath Day?" (v. 17) "You are not to give your daughters in marriage to their sons, nor are you to take their daughters in marriage for your sons or for yourselves" (v. 25).

Second, Nehemiah *reminded* them of examples from the past of people who had disobeyed. He pointed out their ancestors (see v. 18), who because of disobedience regarding the Sabbath, ended up in Babylonian captivity. He also reminded them of Solomon's downfall (see v. 26). Even though Solomon was the wisest and one of the godliest kings in Israel's history, his foreign wives led him into idolatry and brought tragedy to the whole nation.

How often have you learned from the mistakes of biblical characters? Recently, as I was speaking at a retreat in east Texas, the Lord convicted me again as I challenged the women with the example of Martha. The Lord did not rebuke Martha for her busyness but for her attitude. Luke 10:40 says that "Martha was distracted by all the preparations that had to be made." Her distraction led to indignation, and she criticized, "Lord, don't You care that my sister has left me to do the work by myself? Tell her to help me!" I have to pray that I don't become distracted from my primary focus on Christ. I become more critical of others when I take my eyes off Christ. There is nothing wrong with work, but there is everything wrong with a critical spirit which keeps us from worshiping the Lord with a grateful heart. If one must be a "Martha," it is important to be a "Martha" with a "Mary" attitude.

Because of the people's rebellious state, Nehemiah next *restored* the temple. He ordered that the rooms be purified for proper use again. He also restored the Levites to their rightful positions, and all of Judah brought the tithes to help support them. Trustworthy officials were placed in charge of the distribution of the supplies.

Since the people had profaned the Sabbath, Nehemiah restored the Sabbath rest by ordering the Levites to purify themselves and to guard the gates in order to preserve the sanctity of the Sabbath. They forbade merchants to bring merchandise into the city to sell on the Sabbath.

When Nehemiah discovered that many Jews had married foreigners, he rather forcefully made them vow that their children would not marry foreigners. Just as Tobiah had gained a foothold in the temple, so had Sanballat: Sanballat's daughter had married a son of Joiada, one of the sons of Eliashib the priest. Nehemiah chased Sanballat's son-in-law from the temple, then purified the priests and the Levites of everything foreign.

The Book of Nehemiah begins and ends with Nehemiah praying. What a challenge to us that in every circumstance of life we need to be on our knees. In Nehemiah 13, he asked three times that God remember him and his deeds (vv. 14, 22, 31)—not because he felt God might forget him but in order that God would bless his efforts to reform the Israelites. He knew that ultimate revival in the heart comes from God.

ADDING REINFORCEMENT

As the Israelites heard God's Word (including the prayers of leaders from the past), they were greatly challenged. One way to challenge your prayer life to greater growth is to study some of the great prayer warriors of the Bible. Following is a suggested list for your consideration:

- Moses (Deuteronomy 9:26-29)
- Hannah (1 Samuel 1:26-28)
- Jehoshaphat (2 Chronicles 20:5-12)
- Jeremiah (Jeremiah 17:7-18)
- Mary (Luke 1:46-55)
- Paul (Ephesians 1:15-21; Philippians 1:9-11; Colossians 1:9-12; 1 Thessalonians 3:9-13; Hebrews 13:20-21)

MAINTAINING DAILY UPKEEP

If you have accepted Christ as your Savior, how are you growing spiritually? Read a passage each day about holy living, then write a journal entry under *Applying God's Word* on how it could challenge you to mature spiritually. Memorize and recite 2 Corinthians 7:1 daily.

Day 1   Approaching God's Word: John 17:17; Hebrews 4:12-13; 7:26-27

Applying God's Word:

Memorizing God's Word: 2 Corinthians 7:1

Day 2   Approaching God's Word: 1 Peter 1:2, 14-16; 4:2
Applying God's Word:

Day 3   Approaching God's Word: Romans 12:1-2
Applying God's Word:

Day 4   Approaching God's Word: 1 John 2:15-17
Applying God's Word:

Day 5   Approaching God's Word: 1 John 3:1-3

Applying God's Word:

Day 6   Approaching God's Word: Ephesians 4:20-24
         Applying God's Word:

Day 7   Approaching God's Word: Colossians 3:9-17
         Applying God's Word:

Building Block Principles for My Life

INTRODUCTION

If you are leading a group through the study of the Book of Nehemiah, you are in for an enriching adventure. As you take the members through the *Group Participation* section, do so in sequence. You will lead them in discussing key questions (though not every question) asked in the inductive study *(Gathering the Materials)*, plus follow-up questions or activities.

Tips for Leaders
Preparation

❦ Pray for the Holy Spirit's guidance as you prepare, so you will be equipped to lead the lesson and make it applicable. Pray for your participants personally; ask God to help them as they work through the study prior to the session; and pray for the meeting's impact.

❦ Gather and/or prepare any materials you or the group will need.

❦ Read through the entire lesson and related Scriptures. Answer the questions for yourself.

The Meeting

❦ Start and end on time.

❦ Have group members wear name tags during meetings until they know one another's names.

❦ Spend the first 5–15 minutes of the initial meeting introducing yourselves, if this is necessary. Otherwise, spend some time answering an icebreaker question (see samples below). In fact, you may use any good activity to help members get acquainted, interact with each other, or feel that they belong.

Icebreaker Questions

Icebreakers help your people become better acquainted over the course of the study. If the group members don't know each other well, choose questions that are general or nonthreatening. As time goes by, questions may become more specific or focused. Reassure the members that they may pass on any question they feel is too personal. Choose from these samples or create your own.

> *What do you like to do for fun?*
> *What is your favorite season? Dessert? Book?*
> *What would be your ideal vacation?*
> *What exciting thing happened to you this week?*
> *What was the most memorable activity you did with your family when you were a child?*
> *Name three things you are thankful for.*
> *Imagine that your home is on fire. What three items would you try to take with you as you escaped?*
> *If you were granted one wish, what would you wish?*
> *Name the quality you appreciate most in a friend.*
> *What is your pet peeve?*
> *What is your greatest hope? Greatest fear?*
> *What has been your greatest accomplishment? Greatest disappointment?*

The Discussion

In discussion, members should interact not only with you, the group leader, but with one another. Usually you will start the ball rolling by asking a question to which there is more than one single acceptable answer. You are also responsible for keeping the discussion on track because if it gets out of hand and rambles, it loses much of its value.

Here are some guidelines for leading discussion:

❦ Maintain a relaxed, informal atmosphere.

❦ Encourage everyone to take part, but don't call on people by name unless you are sure they are willing to participate.

❦ Give members enough time to reflect and answer a question. If necessary, restate it.

❦ If someone is shy, ask that person to answer an opinion question or another nonthreatening question.

❦ Acknowledge any contribution, regardless of merit.

❦ Don't correct or embarrass a person who gives a wrong answer.

Thank the person; then ask, "What do the rest of you think?"

❦ If someone monopolizes the discussion, say, "On the next question, let's hear from someone who hasn't spoken yet." Or sit next to the monopolizer to avoid encouraging her with eye contact.

❦ If someone goes off on a tangent, wait for the person to draw a breath, then say, "Thanks for those interesting comments. Now let's get back to . . . " and mention the subject under consideration; or ask or restate a question that will bring the discussion back on target.

❦ If someone asks a question, allow others in the group to give their answers before you offer yours.

❦ Summarize the discussion after the contributions cease and before you move on.

❦ Include in your meeting a time for sharing lessons which group members learn in their personal study time, praise items, prayer requests and answers, as well as a time for prayer itself.

PRAYING PURPOSEFULLY

OBJECTIVE

To encourage group members to put their problems into perspective with prayer.

PREPARATION

Bring paper and pencils for the group.

GROUP PARTICIPATION

1. Ask:

    🐝 *Where is your childhood home?*

    🐝 *Have you ever been homesick for it? If so, to what degree? Share the circumstances.*

Say: **Though Nehemiah had never lived in Jerusalem, he was concerned about the Jewish homeland and longed to go there. One might say that he was homesick for Jerusalem.**

2. Have group members share their answers and insights from question 2 in *Gathering the Materials*.

3. Invite members to share responses to questions 4 and 5. Call for other character traits of God not included in the given Scriptures.

4. Distribute paper and pencils and direct group members to write their own prayers, using the perfect pattern of Nehemiah's prayer: praise, penitence, promises remembered, and petition. After a few minutes, ask if anyone would like to share her prayer to encourage the others.

5. Have the group members share their answers to question 9. Ask: **What do you consider success?**

6. Have group members share their responses to question 10.

7. Say: **At the bottom of the paper on which you wrote your prayer, name one person or cause for which you are burdened to pray. Commit to pray daily for the remainder of the study of Nehemiah.** (Note: If your group meets weekly for the eight studies in this book, the members will pray for approximately as long as it took to rebuild the Jerusalem wall–52 days.) Urge members to accept this challenge. God can do even what seems impossible.

8. Invite volunteers to share the building block principles they wrote for Nehemiah 1 on page 75. Encourage members to appreciate the insights that are different than their own.

9. Ask if any group members have something they want to share about following the prayer suggestions in *Adding Reinforcement* or about ways they were encouraged by God's Word, from *Maintaining Daily Upkeep*.

10. Divide the members into pairs. Challenge them to quote to one another the Scripture memory verses, 2 Peter 1:3-4.

11. To close, direct members to pray together in pairs, asking the Lord to help their partners put their problems into perspective with prayer.

PLANNING PATIENTLY

OBJECTIVE
To encourage prayerful waiting for God's perfect timing.

PREPARATION
1. Think of a time in your life when God's answer to your prayer exceeded your initial request.
2. Bring a clock to the meeting.

GROUP PARTICIPATION
1. Before the members arrive, place the clock so that it will face them. Deliberately take your time getting set up for the meeting so that members have to wait and watch the clock. Finally ask: **Are you tired of waiting?** They will probably understand when you say: **Nehemiah had to wait four months until God answered the prayer we studied last session. Today we'll find out what he did during his wait.**
2. Have members describe times when they had to wait for something special to happen. Make sure they tell how long they had to wait and whether or not they were patient.
3. Ask: **What are some benefits of having to wait?**
4. Have a volunteer read Nehemiah 2:1-10 while others follow in their Bibles.
5. Have group members share their responses to question 4.
6. Say: **In Nehemiah 2:4, we read that Nehemiah prayed a spontaneous prayer. Relate a time when you shot an "arrow" prayer that God answered.**
7. Have group members share insights gained from question 6.
8. Read Ephesians 3:20 aloud for the group. Ask:
    ☙ *What does this verse mean to you?*
    ☙ *How did God do "immeasurably more" for Nehemiah?*
    ☙ *Can you share a time in your life when God's answer to your prayer exceeded your original request. (Be prepared to share yourself.)*
9. Ask for volunteers to share the building block principles they wrote for Nehemiah 2:1-10 on page 75.

10. Ask if anyone wants to share any experiences about the prayer suggestions (*Adding Reinforcement*) or how God's Word encourages her (*Maintaining Daily Upkeep*).
11. Divide the members into pairs. Challenge them to quote to one another the Scripture memory verse, 2 Chronicles 7:14.
12. Say: **Think silently of a situation for which you are waiting for God's answer.** After a short while, close with this prayer:

Lord, please help us to wait patiently for Your perfect answers to our prayers. Help us not to be manipulative. Rather, help us to plan as Nehemiah did—in prepartion for Your response. Help us to gladly accept Your will. In Jesus' name,

Amen.

PERCEIVING PROBLEMS PROPERLY

OBJECTIVE

To see God's strength as well as solutions to our problems through solitude with Him.

PREPARATION

1. Bring pictures of a caterpillar and a butterfly.
2. Secure a map of Old Testament Jerusalem on which you can trace Nehemiah's route as he inspected the remains of the wall.
3. Decide which of the psalms assigned for reading in *Maintaining Daily Upkeep* encouraged you the most.

GROUP PARTICIPATION

1. Have group members share their responses to question 1.
2. Read Nehemiah 2:11-20 aloud for the group.
3. Display the pictures of the caterpillar and butterfly. Ask:
   * *What happens between the caterpillar and butterfly stages?*
   * *What are the advantages of going through that stage?*
   * *If you could crawl into a "cocoon," how would you like to emerge?*
4. Have group members give insights gained from question 3.
5. If you found a map of ancient Jerusalem, show the group members Nehemiah's route while inspecting the walls.
6. Have group members share their answers to question 5, especially how someone motivated them without using external rewards.
7. Say: **We all face opposition in some form or another during our lives. Can you think of some types of opposition we might experience?**
8. Ask group members to discuss their answers to question 6.
9. Say: **I'm sure you've all been encouraged this week as you've read the psalms in the *Maintaining Daily Upkeep* section. Who would like to share with the group the psalm which encouraged you the most, and why?** (Be prepared to share yourself.)
10. Invite volunteers to share the building block principles they wrote for Nehemiah 2:11-20 on page 75.

11. Ask if anyone wants to share any experiences about the prayer suggestions *(Adding Reinforcement)* or how God's Word encourages her *(Maintaining Daily Upkeep)*.
12. Divide the members into pairs. Challenge them to quote to one another the memory verses, Psalm 1:1-2.
13. Challenge each person to pray silently in solitude asking the Lord to show her how to perceive her problems through God's eyes.

Leader's Guide 4

PULLING TOGETHER POWERFULLY

OBJECTIVE
To realize the spiritual strength in pulling together and praying for one another.

PREPARATION
1. With contributions from your members, you will either create a fruit salad or a floral bouquet — you decide which. Then call group members and assign each to bring either one piece of fruit or one flower to the meeting. For the sake of variety or uniformity, decide who will bring what before you call. Do not tell the members what the pieces of fruit (or flowers) are for.
2. If members are bringing flowers, supply a vase. If they are donating pieces of fruit, bring a large bowl, plus plates, forks, and knives if the group will eat the fruit salad in the meeting.
3. Recall a time when you were discouraged while trying to complete a task.

GROUP PARTICIPATION
1. Set the large bowl in the middle of the group. After the group members have placed the sliced pieces of fruit in the bowl, make a fruit salad. If you are making a floral bouquet, place the flowers in a vase of water. Decide by some type of drawing which member will take the bouquet home with her.

    Say: **On a small scale today, we have all "pulled together" our resources to complete one simple project. Nehemiah 3–4 will show how the Jews around Jerusalem pulled together to rebuild the wall around Jerusalem.**
2. Have group members share their answers to questions 1–3.
3. Ask: **What kinds of opposition to spiritual growth do Christians face today? What are some examples?**
4. Ask group members to share insights gained from questions 4 and 5.
5. Ask:
    🍃 *When have you become discouraged while trying to complete a*

87

project? (Be prepared to share yourself.)

❦ *How has studying Nehemiah 4 this week encouraged you?*

6. Say: **In Nehemiah 4:9, we read that the Israelites prayed and "posted a guard" for each other.** Ask:

    ❦ *How might we "post a guard" for another person facing opposition?*

    ❦ *When has someone "posted a guard" for you?*

7. Have group members share responses to questions 6 and 7.

8. Say that anyone who wishes may share the building block principle she wrote for Nehemiah 3–4 on page 75.

9. Ask if anyone wants to share any experiences about the prayer suggestions (*Adding Reinforcement*) or how God's Word encourages her to persevere (*Maintaining Daily Upkeep*).

10. Divide the members into pairs. Challenge them to quote to one another the memory verse, Galatians 6:9.

11. If it would be comfortable for the group, have them join hands and pray conversationally (in short sentences) asking the Lord to pull them together as a group to glorify the Lord. Have them name a person they will "post a guard" for during the next week.

PREVAILING AGAINST OPPOSITION

OBJECTIVE
To realize that we can face and conquer all kinds of opposition—internal and external—with the Lord's strength.

PREPARATION
Recall a never-ending project of yours that was finally finished due to the Lord's intervention.

GROUP PARTICIPATION
1. Read Nehemiah 5:1-5. Ask: **How do the problems of the passage compare to problems in today's society? Are there similarities or differences?**
2. Have group members share their answers to questions 2 and 5.
3. Refer to the four plots (mentioned in *Laying the Foundation*) that the enemies used against Nehemiah to try to stop the progress of building the wall; namely, distraction (6:1-4), defamation (6:5-9), disobedience (6:10-13), and discouragement (6:17-19).
   Ask: **Which plot would have most easily tricked you? Why?**
4. Have group members respond to question 9.
5. Say: **Nehemiah 6:15 tells that the wall was completed in 52 days.** Ask: **Why do you think the Jews were able to complete the wall in such a short time?**
6. Have group members share answers to question 10.
7. Ask: **Which psalm from** *Maintaining Daily Upkeep* **ministered to you the most? Why?**
8. Call for volunteers to share the building block principles they wrote for Nehemiah 5–6 on page 75.
9. Ask if anyone wants to share any experiences about the prayer suggestions (*Adding Reinforcement*) or how she will depend more on the Lord (*Maintaining Daily Upkeep*).
10. Divide the members into pairs. Challenge them to quote to one another the memory verse, 1 John 4:4.

PUTTING A PRIORITY ON GOD'S WORD

OBJECTIVE
To place a priority on God's Word and on praising Him.

PREPARATION
1. Write a prayer to God portraying your spiritual pilgrimage.
2. Recall a time when you were filled with great joy because you had been obedient to God.
3. Bring paper and pencils for the group.

GROUP PARTICIPATION
1. Ask group members to share their answers to question 1 about standing still on their feet for long periods of time. Say: **I would venture to guess that few of us stood still as long as the Israelites did when they listened to the reading of God's Word.** Have a volunteer read aloud Nehemiah 8:1-6.
2. Have group members share insights gained from questions 2 and 3.
3. Say: **You've heard of the term "old-fashioned camp meeting." Perhaps the idea originated with the Israelites. Let's see what you found out about their camp meeting from answering question 4.** Let members share their responses.
4. Say: **You read the prayer in 9:5-37 in the course of completing the inductive study.** Ask:
   ❦ *What impressed you the most about the prayer?*
   ❦ *How would you describe God's character?*
5. Say: **The Israelites were repentant for their sins, as we see in 8:9 and 9:3. True repentance requires a turning away from sin and a turning to what is right.** Ask: **How has God turned your life around or the life of someone you know?**
6. Have group members share answers to question 8.
7. Say: **As a result of their repentance and obedience, the Israelites were full of great joy, as we read in 8:10, 12, 17; and 9:4-5. Ask: Could you share about a time when, because you were obedient, you were full of great joy?** (Be prepared to share yourself.)

8. Give each person paper and a pencil. Say: **This week I have written a prayer, similar in format to the prayer of Nehemiah 9, portraying my own spiritual pilgrimage. I'd like you to take five minutes now** (or more, if time allows) **to do the same. I'm praying that it will be a rewarding experience for you.**

9. Ask for a few volunteers to share their prayers with the others. Begin by reading your own prayer.

10. Invite volunteers to read the building block principles they wrote for Nehemiah 8–9 on page 75.

11. Ask if anyone wants to share any experiences about the prayer suggestions *(Adding Reinforcement)* or how God's Word encourages her *(Maintaining Daily Upkeep)*.

12. Divide the members into pairs. Challenge them to quote to one another the memory verses, Psalm 119:1-2.

13. Close in prayer asking the Lord to help group members put a priority on knowing and obeying God's Word.

PROMISING OBEDIENCE PENITENTLY

OBJECTIVE

To encourage group members to make a penitent promise of obedience to God.

PREPARATION

1. Bring an item that has your signature on it (for example, charge card, library card, driver's license, or social security card).
2. Read Psalms 38 and 51 and write down verses that represent genuine repentance.
3. Recall Bible characters who demonstrated true repentance for their sins.
4. Bring paper and pencils for the group.

GROUP PARTICIPATION

1. Hold up the item with your signature on it. Say: **You'd be surprised how many times you have signed your name on documents. If you don't believe it, take out your purses or billfolds to see how many times or in how many places you can find your signature. Who has the most?** Give a round of applause to the person with the most personal signatures. Ask: **To what kind of document did the Israelites mentioned in Nehemiah 10 sign their names?**
2. Read Nehemiah 9:1-3, 33 aloud. Ask:
   - *In what kind of attitude did the Israelites approach writing the agreement with God?*
   - *What do you think genuine repentance involves?*
   - *Can you name other Bible characters who were genuinely repentant of their sins?* (Supplement members' answers as needed. If they do not think of David, give him as an example. Read portions of Psalms 38 and 51 which prove this.)
3. Have group members share their answers to questions 3 and 4.
4. Ask: **As Christians, we consider Sunday as our Sabbath day because that was the day of Jesus' resurrection. How do you think our present-day society regards the Sabbath rest?**

5. Ask: **Could you tell about a time when being obedient to a rule or law gave you peace?**
6. Have group members respond to questions 7–9.
7. Distribute paper and pencils. Say: **I challenge you to take the next few minutes to think of three ways in which you need to be more obedient to God. And though He doesn't need written and signed documents from us, write an agreement which names the three ways, beginning "Dear God, I promise to . . ."**
8. Say that anyone who wishes may share the building block principle she wrote for Nehemiah 10–11 on page 75.
9. Ask if anyone wants to share any experiences about the prayer suggestions (*Adding Reinforcement*) or how she feels led by God to serve (*Maintaining Daily Upkeep*).
10. Divide the members into pairs. Challenge them to quote to one another the memory verses, Matthew 23:11-12.
11. Ask a member to close in prayer. Let the prayer focus be on seeking strength from the Lord to keep the promises of obedience made in the group.

PURIFYING OURSELVES FOR SERVICE

OBJECTIVE
To strive for purity and obedience in our lives.

PREPARATION
1. Bring a white cloth which you have smudged with soil to the meeting.
2. Also bring a small amount of bleach, a bowl or bucket, and some rubber gloves.

GROUP PARTICIPATION
1. Start the meeting by showing the soiled cloth. Place it in the bowl or bucket and carefully pour the bleach over the stain. The bleach should remove the dirt. Say: **When God purifies something or someone, He does it perfectly. No stains or smudges remain. Today we will learn the significance of purification in the Book of Nehemiah and how it can relate to us today.**
2. Have group members share responses to question 2.
3. Read Hebrews 10:14 aloud. Ask: **What do you think it means to be "made holy"?** Have volunteers read aloud Romans 12:1-2; 2 Corinthians 7:1; and 1 John 2:15-17. Ask: **What do these passages have to say regarding holy living?**
4. Have group members share responses to questions 4, 6, and 7.
5. Invite volunteers to share the building block principles they wrote for Nehemiah 12–13 on page 75.
6. Ask: **As you review the building block principles from Nehemiah that we came up with as a group, which one do you feel challenges you the most? Why?**
7. Divide the members into pairs. Challenge them to quote to one another the memory verse, 2 Corinthians 7:1.
8. Ask if anyone wants to share any experiences about the prayer suggestions (*Adding Reinforcement*) or how God's Word encourages her (*Maintaining Daily Upkeep*).
9. Have members pray with their partners for continuing life changes after the study of Nehemiah concludes.

10. Close in prayer thanking the Lord for all the lessons from Nehemiah that the group has learned.